D0017958

HOW
TO LIVE AN
AWESOME
LIFE

HOW TO LIVE AN AWESOME LIFE

HOW TO LIVE WELL, DO GOOD, BE HAPPY

BY POLLY CAMPBELL

EDITIONS

Published in the United States by Viva Editions, an imprint of Start Midnight LLC, 101 Hudson Street, Thirty-Seventh Floor, Suite 3705, Jersey City, NJ 07302.

Printed in the United States.
Cover design: Scott Idleman/Blink
Text design: Frank Wiedemann

First Edition
10 9 8 7 6 5 4 3 2 1

Trade paper ISBN: 978-1-63228-033-6
E-book ISBN: 978-1-63228-037-4

Library of Congress Cataloging-in-Publication Data is available on file.

Jerry, thanks for all the little things—the coffee and the calls, the laundry and the late-night conversations, and the countless other things you do to make a big, fat, awesome difference in my life.

Piper, you have showed me how to climb trees, how to sing while doing math equations, and how to appreciate millipedes and moths and worms. In a gazillion ways, you show me what awesome looks like.

Thank you Team Neubert.

ACKNOWLEDGMENTS

From the time I was a kid growing up in Seaside, a small town on the north Oregon Coast, to now, I've been surrounded and supported by awesome people who have loved me well and made me better. I would not be here without them, and this book wouldn't be either.

To my parents, Lynda and Steve Campbell; my sister, Paige Campbell; and my awesome nephew, Quinn McCarthy; thank you. I love you.

To my awesome friends Sherri Sacconaghi and Tonya Robson, thanks for the love and encouragement, fun and humor. Thanks, too, to Todd, Luke, and Kyler Robson.

Thanks to Regina Micheline-Eldien, Teresa Adams, Lori Wampler, Kelly Hatler, and Megan Thatcher.

To Ginger Buzzell, president (and only member) of the Polly Campbell Fan Club, your positive energy and encouragement inspires me. Thank you.

To friends and writers Jodi Helmer and Kelly James Enger, thanks for your insight, both professionally and personally. And, Jeff Mazeriak, thanks for your encouragement and wisdom.

To the extraordinary Brenda Knight, thanks for everything you bring. Thank you as well to Eileen Duhné. To Katie Gira, thanks for saving me from myself and to the entire Viva Editions team thanks for bringing awesome to the world.

To the booksellers who have embraced my books and to all of you who have read my work, or reached out to me via the Internet or through my appearances, workshops, and other events, I am so grateful. Thank you for sharing your experiences with me. Everything I write, I write with you in mind—no kidding. It is a privilege to connect with you personally in the process. Thanks for sharing all this with me.

TABLE OF CONTENTS

INTRODUCTION

I was fifteen minutes late even before I hopped into the rented Hyundai and jammed the pedal down. And, well, nothing says speed quite like a Hyundai. The engine whined up the highway ramp from Corte Madera and onto the Golden Gate Bridge. Sweat was already beading along my hairline when the traffic came to a stop. A complete, turn-off-the-ignition-you-aren't-going-anywhere kind of stop.

I looked at the cars, stopped in every lane; looked at my watch; yep, still late—and then I looked beyond. I was stopped on the Golden Gate Bridge. In its center. Overlooking the abalone-colored bay on a clear, warm fall day at sunset. It was stunning, this view. This weather. The sea below. The sun bouncing off the bridge. And in that instant, the moment transformed from a tight and stressful I'm-gonna-be-late occasion to one filled with all kinds of awesome.

Life is like that. There are awesome moments—the kind that cause our jaws to drop, tears to well up, and love and gratitude to pulse through our beings—right there in the middle of the congested, icky ones.

And if we are paying attention and engaged in our lives, those moments of beauty can intermingle with those moments of ick and raise us up a little. They can inspire us. Encourage us. Change our lives.

That kind of energy—the energy of awe—can remind us of our purpose, motivate us to live our passions, move us toward a life of meaning. That kind of energy illuminates life during the big experiences and the quiet little moments. It clarifies our vulnerabilities and weaknesses—for sure, because awe can remind us how small we really are—but in the very same instant, it connects us to the bigger things in life and to our vast inner landscape. The place where joy and possibility reside no matter what we encounter in the outer world.

Thing is, we don't often see it. We don't pay attention to this energy. We forget to slow down and look for those transcendent moments. We're just too busy. Or we turn away. Or we think it's indulgent to pause for a breath, or read a book that moves us, or savor our food, and marvel at the world around us. So we forget to see the goodness that is there and has been there all along.

We notice, instead, what is hard. We complain. Worry. Zone out. Eat too much. We focus on not getting sick instead of living healthy. You see the distinction? Life is all of it, of course—the sickness and the health, the messy and the pristine—so we must notice all of it. Sure, we see the traffic jam, but we must also look at the view beyond.

When we can do this, we become less snarky. More generous. We become healthier and happier, more patient, less stressed. We inspire and become inspired.

Of course, there is plenty that is awful—as in rotten—rather than awesome in this world. Awe, or in its archaic Scandinavian form of Old Norse, was used in that language to describe fear. In ancient Greek the word derived from *akhos,* which meant "pain."

Awe became regularly associated with the gods; fearsome, omniscient, punishing gods and rulers.

Technically, to say that something is awful is to say that it is full of awe, which is the feeling we get when we are bowled over by something amazing and big and unexplainable. That's the feeling we get when we stare at the full moon over the Rocky Mountains or watch a spider weave its web.

But these days the word awful has been co-opted to imply something terrible. Dreadful. Something so scary or horrific that we are appalled, shocked, devastated by the sheer badness of it all.

Awful stuff nowadays means bombs that can bring down towers of concrete and steel. Mutant cells that replicate so fast they can kill us in months; love that once infused every breath dissipating into emptiness in just a few years' time; the loss of a job after thirty years; a hurricane with ninety-mile-per-hour winds and thirty-foot waves—all awful.

We wouldn't say that those things are awesome, no, but they contain the seeds of awe just the same. Think of the awesome and sometimes awful power of Mother Nature. Both words are impressive, both are awe-filled, but one surrounds you with its mysticism and possibility and beauty. The other scares the beje-ezus out of you.

When I talk about awesome, I'm taking the more benevolent, marvelous view of the word. After all, I'm part of the generation that made "totally awesome" into a tagline. First popularized in the late '60s and '70s, the term became popular as slang for "excellent" and was often associated with the California surfers who used it to describe primo surfing waves. It didn't hurt that movie characters like Spicoli, played by Sean Penn in *Fast Times at Ridgemont High,* batted the word around on the big screen: "Awesome, dude."

When I talk of awe, I'm talking about wonder. About accessing the amazing. I'm using the word to express reverence, admiration. Awe like this can show up in every aspect of our lives—even the parts we think of as not so great.

When we can look at all aspects of our lives with this kind of wonder and admiration, awe changes us. We are broken open by it. It forces us to rethink things. To tweak our behaviors and choices. To move toward things that matter.

Psychologist Nicholas Humphrey says that awe forces us to reconfigure our mental model so we can make sense of what we've seen and experienced. It broadens us, inspires us.

Awe, then, has the ability to awaken us. It can show us the beauty that already exists and remind us who we are at our spiritual core. It brings us closer to our purpose and passion and helps us create meaning. It helps us to live with the mystery in life, to survive the uncertainty of it all. It allows us to sink into the expe-

rience of living. To engage in it. To be touched by it. To participate rather than needing to manipulate, contrive, or control every
moment.

When you live in awe of your life, you are open to diverse
experiences. Some are easy-peasy, comfortable, and even joyous.
Others totally suck. But you can be okay because you know that
every experience is multi-dimensional and that the possibilities
are limitless. Life is never just one thing. It is always more than
bad or good.

I once spent an hour watching two sliver-sized ants move a dead
bee, probably a hundred times their size, half a block. I'm nerdy
like that. Course, I had plenty of other things to do, yet I was
transfixed by these little creatures. I was in awe.

You've got better things to do, right? What a time suck,
watching those ants. Right. All true. But I cannot tell you how
often I think of those ants. I marvel at their tenacity. The awesome
task they took on without any quit.

When I'm under pressure and feeling stressed, I think about
what the ants accomplished in that hour and how hard they
worked and how they were wired to succeed. Then I marvel at the
fact that this is true for all of us. We are all wired to succeed, to live
purposeful lives.

That's just it: When we experience awe, we transform the
moment into something better. But we've got to go after it. Slow
down long enough to look at the cracks in the sidewalk, to see the
cracks in our own lives and find the amazing there too. This isn't
something you wait for; it's something you explore and uncover
and discover both within yourself and outside.

Too often we think that our own awesome exists only in the
easy moments when our expectations are met and our dreams come
true. So we overlook the ants. We judge them and walk over them,
deeming them irrelevant to our lives, and we miss the moment and
the awe that permeates everything.

This keeps us stuck. It prevents us from fully engaging in life until that One Big Moment comes, the one we think will change everything.

"When I just get the job, everything will be awesome."

"When he finally proposes, our relationship will be better."

"When I just get healthier, thinner, richer, life will be great."

Baloney. That's not how it works. When we attach to external outcomes and wait for life to change before we feel joy or greatness or success, we will spend a lifetime waiting for the goodness to appear. But when we can see the awesome already out there, in every moment, we create more of it in our experience. Right now.

This is how it works. This is how to live an awesome life.

Awesome emanates from your very core. You are undeniably awesome, right now. Don't believe it? Think for one second about what it takes for your physical body to survive this moment; the systems that are required to work in unison to keep you alive. You, my friend, are nothing short of awesome, even as you sit there eating those Cheetos. It's just a matter of whether you are brave enough to unleash all that awesomeness to create your best life. One that is meaningful and bold.

In these next pages I'll offer a game plan for how to do it. This book is about how we can uncover the awesome within us—the stuff that's already there—and experience the wonder beyond us. It's about how we can cultivate awe in our own lives to expand, through awareness and intuition and authenticity, into wholeness. It's about how awe can illuminate our purposes and passions.

I'll share some stories of others who created awesome lives. Each chapter also offers practices you can do in five minutes or less, as well as some longer journaling exercises and activities designed to help you engage with the awesome qualities of your life.

Do the exercises if you want—or not. Read this book chapter by chapter or go to the section that will help you most right now. Take what works and discard the rest. You will not be graded on how well you use this book. You won't be judged.

Living an awesome life isn't about following a strict set of rules.

It's about living from your essence and using that authenticity to catapult you into your best life. What that life looks like is up to you. You are the creator of your moments. They are shaped by what you believe, what you notice, how you behave. You get to choose.

I will tell you this, and I wholly and completely believe it: No matter who you are, what you've done, where you've been, or what you've experienced and borne, the very next moment can be awesome.

Seriously. Sounds a little woo-woo, I know, but this is totally doable. When you discover the awe in the now, it transforms the next moment and makes it more possible, a bit easier to bear. A bit more awesome.

When you string together a whole batch of little awesome moments, you can create a big, fat, awesome life. Starting now. From right here.

This is what I'm working on too. This is what I'm after—making the best of the moments I have, no matter how they show up. This is how to live an awesome life. You ready?

CHAPTER 1

BECOMING AWARE OF AWESOME

■ ■ ■

*I was struck by the fact that I hadn't been awed in a while.
Did that mean awesome things had disappeared from
my life? No. What it did mean was that I'd gotten too
caught up in distractions and mind mucking to recognize
anything as awe-inspiring.... I hadn't been paying attention to the beauty around me.*

—SUE PATTON THOELE

When I was twenty-two years old, roughly a billion years ago, I sat
in Naples, Italy, eating pizza in a centuries-old stone-walled restaurant said to be the birthplace of pizza. It was raining outside and
we were warmed by the enormous brick ovens in the narrow shop.

Pretty sure the sauce was simply a mix of fresh, pureed tomatoes with a bit of basil and garlic and parsley, spread lightly over the
thin crust. The topping was fresh mozzarella and tomatoes lightly
tossed on, not blanketed across like the thick pies in U.S. pizzerias.
I was sharing this pizza, this moment, with my best friend. And
pizza never tasted so good.

In that moment, I felt connected not only to everyone in that
shop, but to all who had ever eaten pizza in that place in the centu-

ries before, and to everyone, anywhere, who'd ever eaten pizza.

For just a moment, I was completely present and connected. This simple yet sublime pizza-eating experience elevated my experience of the world. It changed how I thought about people everywhere. For just an instant, while eating my slice, I experienced the emotion of awe.

WHAT IS AWE?

It's easy to think of awe when we are watching the sun sink below the horizon over the ocean, or when we are gazing at a newborn baby. But awe is accessible in the pizza-eating moments and tiny details of our lives too.

Neuropsychologist Paul Pearsall called awe our eleventh emotion and described it as an "overwhelming and bewildering sense of connection with a startling universe that is usually far beyond the narrow band of our consciousness."

Others who study the emotion talk about it in terms of admiration, reverence, and elevation. Awe stirs that sense that there is something greater than the self. According to psychologists Dacher Keltner and Jonathan Haidt, awe is dependent on two conditions: One, vastness; the sense that there is something bigger. And two, accommodation. When you experience awe, they say, it requires you to change the way you think about the world in order to process or contain the experience. Awe transforms us, opens us up, roots us in the present moment, and changes how we participate in life.

Living with awe, feeling awesome, cultivating awe, and experiencing the awe-inspiring are all about elevating your experience so that you can live your best life. When you cultivate awe in the moments of your life, not only does life become magical and fascinating, but you release your greatest power of love and playfulness and curiosity. To be in awe is to be inspired. To be reverent of all that is. To recognize your own marvelousness and realize your capacity to access your own awesome greatness.

WHY IS AWE AWESOME?

With awe you feel alive, connected, authentic. You feel a part of something bigger. You are instilled with a sense of value and well-being. Life becomes bolder, more vibrant. Those good feelings aren't unfounded.

In one study, Stanford researcher Melanie Rudd found that awe expands our perception of time and creates a sense that we have more of it available. When we feel "time-rich," as she describes it, we are also more likely to seek out experiences and volunteer to help others. Awe also moves us into the present moment and leaves us feeling less stressed, less burdened by time constraints, and overall more satisfied with life.

Psychologist Nicholas Humphrey says that awe offers us a distinct evolutionary advantage. And self-proclaimed global psychologist and philosopher Milan Ljubincic says that awe causes us to feel a sense of "cosmic significance" that "inspires us to thrive and not just survive."

For me, the benefits of awe are even more immediate and practical. When you go looking for awesome, you find it, and that just makes every moment a bit better, less stressful, and more doable. Awe is the thing that helped me see the beauty rather than the hardship when I was stuck in traffic on the Golden Gate Bridge.

When we cultivate awe, we are open to inspiration and possibility. We also tend to make better choices and be more compassionate, open, and responsive rather than reactive.

Awe almost never shows up for me without a side of gratitude. With awe there is also appreciation and the possibility for joy. It leaves the door open to purpose and meaning.

Research by psychologist Michael Steger and others indicates that when we are living purposeful lives, we are happier, more capable and effective. With awe, there is the possibility for an abundance of all of this good stuff in every moment of our lives, even while doing mundane household chores, or while sitting in traffic, or eating pizza.

For just a moment on that murky night in Italy so many years ago, the blend of flavors and aromas and atmosphere was so intense and magnificent that I felt joyous and grateful. I was lost in the sensory experience of it all. I forgot about the tight budget we were traveling on and the weight of my backpack and the homesickness that hit when I was tired. I didn't worry about our plans for the next day. I just fell into that pizza and the experience of eating it with my buddy and the Italians in the shop who were loving it too. And I realized in a big way that we all have the same basic needs. We all need each other. We are all worthy of love and joy. And pizza. The moment was an awesome one.

I felt awe, too, when I sat with my grandmother as she neared death. It was a privilege to be there as her body prepared for the transition. I was in awe of her: the life she had lived and the depth of the love we shared. I sat in utter amazement too of the human body and the way it works and all it does to sustain us on this planet. I was sad. And I was also elevated by the experience of sitting with her.

I've been awed by sunsets. I'm in awe just about every time I see the ocean and hear the smashing waves. And just today, when I was playing with my cat, I watched as his tail curled and batted and communicated, though he was burrowed deep under a pile of newspapers, and I marveled.

You see, the big awesome stuff of our lives often shows up in the little moments. You don't have to visit the Grand Canyon, though it is most definitely awesome, or climb a mountain peak, or eat pizza in Italy, to experience the awe in your life. You can find it in this moment, right now, as soon as you stop doing and start being.

Power Up: Awe is apparent in every aspect of life, in moments both big and small. The key is to cultivate awareness.

WHAT DOES AN AWESOME LIFE LOOK LIKE?

An awesome life isn't pristine or without trouble, but awe-filled people step toward the trouble when it appears. They don't shy away. They know that even moments of fear and pain can be filled with possibility, so they move toward what life offers with courage—even when it offers ick. They may not like it. They may cry and pout and complain, but they are not *stuck* in the pain.

Those who are living awesome lives realize that experience is dynamic and fluid. So they keep going and they pay attention, knowing that nothing is wasted. They immerse themselves in every experience, absorbing the information they need to move forward. They move with compassion, purpose, passion, gratitude, and focus. They use their intuition to navigate the unknown; they hone their awareness and take risks. They live with a positive spirit and seek the awe in the everyday. They are kind and buoyed by the kindness in others. They have fun. They love openly. They laugh often, usually at themselves, and especially when everything just seems too silly and hard and ridiculous. They have the courage to feel small in this vast Universe and to show up in a big way. They are startled and awakened by the wonderfulness of it all. They allow the world to crack them open. To influence and change them.

This is a fun way to live. It's a lighter way to live. It makes times of uncertainty easier to deal with, because even then, we know that possibilities exist beyond our wildest imaginations. This sparks our creativity and optimism, and when we open like this, our potential is unlimited. But to get there, we've got to override our bad-news bias.

LEANING INTO THE DARK

When we are ticked off or lonely or stressed over money or wondering why no one in the entire household is capable of putting toilet paper on the little metal thingy in the bathroom, awe seems obsolete. We rarely feel awe after eating a mongo-sized bag of

M&M's to ease the feelings of insecurity that boil up at work. And when the kids complain about the meal you've just taken an hour to prepare, it's tough to see the moment as an awesome one.

Doesn't help that we are wired with a negativity bias, a tendency to be more intensely influenced by the bad, scary, threatening, or other negative things than by anything else. It's like a personal alarm system that worked well in millennia past, when we had to watch out for poisonous snakes and angry bears and warring clans. This bias made us hyper-aware of danger so that we could survive and respond. Now, though, the biggest threats most of us face are the grocery store running out of ice cream and our spouse stealing the remote.

Still, we are vigilant. We watch for storm warnings in the weather reports and in our lives. Warnings about crime, corruption, costs, cancer, and disease cause us to become consumed by thoughts of what isn't right.

There is plenty that isn't working, sure. Bad stuff does happen, no doubt. But when we are mired in it, we are not in a position to solve those problems. We aren't in a position to heal or make a positive difference. We are too depressed and stressed and scared and worried to take the next best step toward a better place, to even believe there is such a place. As we take a dim view of life, our lives become narrower. We participate less and judge more, and awe becomes something we envy in others.

When we can override our negativity bias and consciously shift into positive emotion, we perform better, even under stress. Barbara Fredrickson, a leading happiness researcher at the University of North Carolina, says that positive emotions expand our attention, our attitudes, and thought patterns, and this in turn heightens our problem-solving abilities and inspires us to take action.

By opting to ease up on our fear-based focus to go looking, instead, for the good stuff, we find more of it. When the dangers do appear, we are more able to deal. We have a lifetime of well-honed skills for dealing with negativity. Now it's time to cultivate the bright-side skills, the things like awe that will help us enjoy this life.

HOW TO BEGIN LIVING AN AWESOME LIFE

Self-awareness and acceptance are two things that can help you live an awesome life. Acceptance is the practice of taking in what is there without judgment, criticism, or resistance.

You don't have to have an opinion. No need to evaluate or criticize. With acceptance, you simply notice what is. You see it. This automatically drops your resistance, which eases a whole bunch of stress right there. When you accept what is, you are not filtering based on what your mom might think, or how it fits some belief etched into you since childhood. You are being present.

Here's how it works. You get up after a rollicking dream and a seven-hour sleep (I know, people, that's not enough) and stumble toward the bathroom. On your way there you catch a glimpse of yourself in the mirror and see that hair. You know what I'm talking about—that pillow-frizzed hair that arrives a full thirty-five seconds before you do. Now, you could look at that hair with fear or disgust. Or you could look at your hair with acceptance and simply state what you see without judgment: *That's my hair.*

When you go with the latter, appreciation often follows, and awe is close on its heels. Because if you stop long enough to notice your hair, you might even marvel at how it just keeps growing without any conscious thought from you—and your heart beats, and your lungs fill, and isn't the body amazing and awesome?

To come at life from a place of resistance or judgment is to be filled with fear. It's constricting. Awe, by its nature, is broadening. When you judge your experience rather than accepting it, you stifle your awareness. Your ability to see the details of your circumstance becomes obscured, one-dimensional. When you mute that judgment, you act with greater openness. Self-awareness grows, illuminating your own beliefs and feelings, needs and desires, strengths and weaknesses—and that illuminates the awesome and everything else.

Power Up: Awe is not the antidote to pain or ugliness or despair. In fact, sometimes it brings it to the forefront— you can be awestruck by the force of a hurricane and still hurting for the people lost in the storm. But when you are able to stop resisting and start accepting what comes into your life, you are able to see it with greater clarity. That allows you to experience awe even during the difficulties. And that ability to see the situation from all sides will help you cope.

TUNING IN TO YOUR OWN AWESOME

We are so obsessed with our to-do lists and with getting everything done that we rarely stop to notice what it is we are doing. Are you acting with compassion? Are you doing things that are meaningful? Are you living an authentic life with purpose and curiosity and joy? Are you cultivating a life filled with awesomeness? Or are you just keeping busy? Going through the motions?

We've all got lots to do—work, chores, family obligations, weekly television dramas. But on my best days—which isn't every day—I act deliberately, instead of by default. I want to be alive and engaged in this life. Play in it. Feel it. Smell it. See it. When you are tuned in and paying attention and participating, awe is everywhere.

It's time to notice. Awe is the antidote to hopelessness and confusion and stress. It is the fuel of inspiration and creativity. It's a way to feel better, to love deeper, to get off the bench and participate in this life. Think of it this way: The fastest way to create your best life, to elevate your experience, is to notice how good it already is. It's time we marvel and wonder and feel the awe.

....

IN THE MOMENT PRACTICE:
SEEK OUT THE BEAUTY

Think of the last time you were moved by an incredibly beautiful scene. This could be something you witnessed in nature, or a wonderful exchange between people—whatever. For two minutes, just sit quietly and think about what you saw. What you felt. Why it touched you so. Let yourself experience the emotions that well up. That is awe. Now carry it with you into the next moment.

....

AWARENESS—THE LAUNCHPAD TO AWE

We've got a little experiment going on around the house these days. The sole objective is to get the folks I live with to pay attention to the place where they are living.

Each day, I change something up in the house where we've lived for ten years. I turn a picture frame upside down; put a fork on the bookshelf when nobody's looking. Once I put my ukulele sheet music where the piano book should be, and a candle with the wooden spoons. Then I wait and see who will notice and when.

My daughter, she's pretty good at this game. This is surprising, since it seems nearly impossible for her to see the bath towel in the middle of the floor, or the empty toilet paper roll on the counter, or the Barbie on the dining room table.

My husband is getting better at it too. Mr. J might miss a cereal box in the cupboard, but the guy has no problem seeing a fork in the flower pot. He is starting to notice the other subtleties of family life too. He's more in tune. The game has helped us look at familiar things in a new way.

It's easy to become blind to the familiar spaces in our lives. We navigate our routine on autopilot, and entire dimensions of our day become invisible.

You get so used to seeing her there at the sink, you don't notice that her hair is a different color today or that she's wearing sadness around her like a cloak. Or you expect to see the brewed coffee each morning, so you forget that he made it just for you, just because he loves you, even though he doesn't even drink coffee.

We fail to see the blooms emerging from the shrub along the front window. We forget to watch as the shadows change along the bookshelf, each day marking the march of winter. But I'll bet you can remember what it feels like to see the first tulip blooming in your yard after a winter with sixty-five inches of snow. We notice those special things. Thing is, life is better when we notice the blooms and the love and the people—all of the time.

Awareness helps us to become present to the life we are leading. It is the antithesis of missing the stoplights on the drive to work. It roots us in the moment and connects us to the planet and the people and the things that we often just walk on by. These, of course, are the things worth noticing, because these things are tethered to awe. When we become more present—engaged in the single moment of our lives that is right now—we also see more to marvel and wonder about. We open the chutes of gratitude and appreciation. Lower the anxiety and stress and depression that can emerge when we are running around busy-like but not present to anything. When we live with awareness of the present moment, the little familiar things that are often invisible become visible again.

THREE WAYS TO PRACTICE MINDFUL AWARENESS

I'm not asking you to meditate for an hour or to move to a monastery. I'm just suggesting you breathe deep and slow down and practice paying attention to this moment now. The practice of mindfulness helps attract awe and peace and clarity and other good stuff. Try it.

1. **Slow down.** Give yourself space. Make time for the pause. Build in a few minutes here and there simply to take a deep breath, sit silently, and take in the moment. I do this between transitions in my day. Before I make the call, or get up to get coffee, or start on a new project, I just pause and pay attention. You'll be surprised by what you discover that's been there all along.

2. **Operate with all of your senses.** Awareness grows when we use *all that we are* to experience the world. Taste it, see it, smell it, hear it, feel it. Notice textures and flavors and feelings and birds chirping in the background. Go beyond what you can see.

3. **Stop doing and start being.** We get so busy marking things off our to-do lists (sometimes I'll even add things to my list just so I can have the joy of marking them off) that we lose sight of what we are actually doing. We got a lot done, for sure, but does any of it matter? Did it excite you? Inspire you? Did it change the world for the better?

To live an awesome life, we must become aware of what we are doing and how we are showing up. Then we can attend to the things that matter most.

CHANGING THE WORLD WITH OUR AWARENESS

I don't think making a positive difference in the world is too lofty a goal. I think it's totally doable for each one of us. Simply by being present, by showing up, we alter the environment around us.

Quantum physics (yep, occasionally I like to sling these fancy-schmanzy science terms around) tells us that the universe changes simply by observation. That all these particles swim around doing their particle thing until somebody pays attention.

The simple act of observing the particles changes their behavior, and that changes our reality, or at least the illusion that we think of as our reality.

If these minute particles of energy are changed when we show up, then we can also change our lives and even the world simply by bringing the highest energy of our being to any situation.

At our core, we are energy sourced by love and compassion and infinite potential. When we become that, our essential nature, when we dial in to who we are, the influence of awesome can extend far and wide.

TUNING IN

This energetic expression can be subtle and simple. It can happen when we look into the eyes of the people we are talking to. When we smile or offer up a handshake or a high five. It happens when we show up and are true and authentic and awesome. But none of that can happen—we cannot feel awe, nor become awe-inspiring until we notice what it is we are doing. When we become aware of how we are behaving and the type of energy we are radiating, we can choose to change it or amp it up.

Last August, my husband took a wilderness survival class. As the group gathered and began getting to know one another, the guide led them up a mountain trail into a heavily wooded area. At the top, he said, "Okay, now, where are you? And where did you come from?"

Few could answer. Mr. J said it was hard to tell where they were because nobody had been paying attention. The group had been so busy talking that they forgot to look around, to take it all in. They forgot to notice. They were already lost in the woods.

We've all been there. Some of us—as in, me—find ourselves in that kind of confusing landscape in small ways every day. Unexpected challenges come up, new people come in, school is cancelled because of snow, and the changes throw us for a loop because we've had our heads down for so long, working or parenting or doing, that we've missed the signs along the way that can better guide us along our path.

....

Be Awesome: *Stop right now, take a deep breath, and direct your attention to your heart. Feel it beating. Listen close to hear its pulse. Imagine that you are looking at it, marveling at its healthy color and strength, and showing it appreciation and love for the job it does 24/7. Connect with your physical core. Notice the awesome that is a part of you, the awesome that sustains you and keeps your body and spirit alive. You are surrounded by awesome. You are awesome. To access all that, move into your heart space and reconnect with all that you are.*

....

When you become aware of what it is you are doing, a couple of things happen. One, you can decide whether it's valuable and either keep on or make a change. And two, you become aware of the choices and opportunities and possibilities that can move you closer to your own passion and purpose, authenticity, and awesomeness.

Once you really see how things are shaping up in the life you are living, you are also more able to see the blessings there. This reminds us that awesome is always present, even during the hard times.

Be deliberate, then, in the things you choose to do. Take notice. Become aware and engage fully, and awareness grows.

Awe starts with awareness, then. But it is cultivated when we allow it to take root in our lives.

....

IN THE MOMENT PRACTICE: ACCEPTING THE GOODNESS

Next time someone gives you a compliment, praise, or appreciation, simply say "Thank you." Don't deflect by saying "Really, I just got lucky today," or shrug your shoulders, or avoid or excuse. Just allow it in. Say "Thank you."

....

ALLOWING THE GOOD STUFF

Awe requires one more step, though. To really experience the awesome in your life, to really raise the level of your life to awesome latitudes, you've got to allow the goodness in. Let it ricochet around the tissues of your heart, settle beneath your skin and in your thoughts. Let awe infuse you, and in return, you get to be fully, marvelously human.

When was the last time you received a compliment and, with your head up, smiled and simply said "Thank you"? Or allowed yourself to cry freely when you were moved to tears by the beauty of the mountains or the sweetness of an elementary school program? When did you last feel softened by the love of an animal, or slow down long enough to feel the sun's heat on the back of your neck?

....

PERENNIAL PRACTICE: TAKING A BREAK

Take a look at your to-do list, or if you're not a crazy list keeper, simply write down five things that you feel you should complete today.

Then, cross out all but three things. Take off the should-do's and the it-would-be-nice-if-I-got-this-done's. Leave only the bare bones, the must-do's.

Now, add one thing to your list simply because you

want to do it. Put down a trip to the Japanese garden, or a quiet lunch while reading a thriller. Maybe you want to go for a run, or take a nap, or call a friend you haven't spoken to in forever.

Put this want-to-do item on your list. Make sure it gets done today. Take your time and notice how good it feels to do something that connects you to the things that make you happy.

Each day, make sure there is at least one thing on your list that is meaningful to you, one thing that is fun or restorative.

....

ESTABLISHING A CULTURE OF AWESOME

The moments that are the most awe-inspiring are often too powerful to fully express with words. But usually we are so moved that we try anyhow. This activates more awe. When we share the experience, researchers say, we actually intensify the good feelings. They bloom into gratitude and compassion and calm.

These things are not contrived. They are already within each of us. Awe simply animates them by reminding us who we are.

Awe is exciting this way. But it's not enough to feel it or think about it—you've got to get moving. You've got to love big—even when people are stupid or you feel vulnerable. Even if they might not love you back. Awe requires you to be brave, open, willing to engage and share. To question and experiment and play and trust, knowing that good is possible even when it's hard to see.

Together, we can do this. We can find our way through all this stuff, the human quirks and qualities that make up our lives. We can allow ourselves to be awakened by awe. To stand up and be bold and weave the awesome moments together to create our lives. It's time. Let's go unleash it.

Power Up: Awe is an emotion that, according to psychologist Nicholas Humphrey, has played a large part in our evolution. It helps us not only to survive but to thrive. But living an awesome life requires action as well as emotion. Awe inspires us to live an awesome life, and that takes a willingness to play.

....

Do Good: *Today, extend empathy and compassion to someone who has really ticked you off. For a moment, put yourself in their shoes and act kindly toward them. You'll both feel better for it.*

....

....

Night Cap: *As you relax at the end of the day or drift off to sleep, make a mental note of awesome moments in your life. Think of a time that tapped your emotions and showed you something new about yourself, a time that touched your soul.*

....

CHAPTER 2:

CREATING YOUR EXPERIENCE

■ ■ ■

Wisdom begins in wonder.

—SOCRATES

I caught a snippet of the Grammy Awards on the night in 2005 when rocker Melissa Etheridge performed. Though Etheridge was bald and physically worn from chemotherapy, her raspy voice ripped through the lyrics "I'm going to show you, baby, that a woman can be tough…" and the rest of the words to the old Janis Joplin tune "Piece of My Heart."

I've forgotten a lot of things in the last ten years, but that single performance, which I watched on our big-box TV, still gives me chills.

Words like *powerful, moving, inspiring*—these come to mind when I try to describe what it was like to see and hear her sing like that. But those adjectives don't even really come close to describing the moment. It was just plain awesome.

I heard Etheridge talk about that performance later. How sick and tired she'd been. How she felt nervous, at first, performing bald. Then how the love from the audience and the music and the moment inspired her. Her sickness was overwhelmed by her passion for the song, her passion for performing.

Her symptoms didn't disappear. But the moment illuminated the talent and strength and resilience that were within her too. In that moment Etheridge chose to create a new experience rather than sit at home complaining about an existing one. In the process, she not only empowered herself, but uplifted the rest of us.

The way to unleash an awesome life isn't simply to notice the awesome that exists all around, but to fully engage in this life, to put yourself out there, and to create the life you desire, full of awesome experiences.

Power Up: To spot the awesome things in your life, you've got to get off the couch, participate, engage, explore. You must be willing to feel deeply, connect with compassion, be open and curious and willing to create.

CAUGHT UP IN COMPLAINT

On the night Etheridge performed, she, like so many of us, had plenty to complain about. Right? You don't have to be a rock star to have health issues or relationship crap. Crazy kids and chaotic schedules and dirty houses and money issues, they plague us all. I'm not even going to talk about gun violence and chemically engineered foods and global warming. Just listing it all out makes me feel tight and stressed. Focus on the negative and you'll find it, and that is a buzzkill.

When we complain—when we repeatedly express our unhappiness—we settle into the place of no solutions and stuckedness. (That's the technical term, by the way.) This is where overwhelm and tension reside, because when we begin ruminating about the bad stuff, it gets bigger, and we feel constricted and narrow. This does not fuel our creativity—which is essential to problem-solving. So instead of figuring out ways to stumble through the muck, instead of coming up with solutions to ease the difficulty, we just keep our steadfast focus on how terrible things are. How busy we are. How tired we are. How broke we are. How fat, lonely, unappreciated we are. Woe is me.

Except it's not. Or it doesn't have to be. I'm not saying to ignore the tough stuff. It's plenty okay to share your frustrations, explain what you don't like, and honestly share what you need. It's even okay to fuss and whine for a few minutes. The road to an awesome life isn't about denying your experience in any way. It's about being open to all of it. When you allow yourself to stay in a cycle of complaint, one of ruminating and blaming, you are not allowing yourself to see the other aspects of your reality—the goodness and love and strength that are there too.

Etheridge's riveting performance didn't cure her cancer, but it reminded us that life isn't one-dimensional. There is never just a single, bad-news story.

Discontent and discomfort are an essential part of life because they provide the contrast. When we are uncomfortable or unhappy, we know what we *don't* want, and that helps us become clear on what it is that we *do* desire. Then we can interrupt the cycle of complaint and start creating the life we want.

BE A CREATOR, NOT A COMPLAINER

The bottle of pinot noir slipped out of the bag just as I stepped into the laundry room. It shattered on the garage step, spitting glass into the hard-to-reach-without-a-long-stick corner by the furnace and into the shoes lined up against the wall. Wine splattered and cascaded down the wall and onto the rubber mat and even up against the front bumper of the car parked a few feet away. Puddles of wine on the step. My first thought was *Dang, that's a darn good bottle of $8.95 wine that I wasted.* The second was *How am I going to clean up this mess?*

The mental complaints were flying faster than I could blink. I had people coming over, a work call to make. I had things to do. I certainly didn't have time for spilled wine. I was veering toward a meltdown. Then I realized something—throwing a fit with red wine trickling down my ankle wasn't going to get it cleaned up. So I grabbed a rag and got to work. Not saying I didn't cuss a little—okay, a lot—but I kept working, and after a few minutes, a basket of rags, and a hose, the garage was clean and it had a nice bouquet.

I became a creator rather than a complainer.

There are going to be entire days of spilled-wine scenarios and messy problems and life's little annoyances, and each time you get to choose: Will you be a creator or a complainer?

Totally up to you.

Power Up: Complaining is a stressful, constrictive pose. Creating is expansive and attitude-opening. If you've got a challenge or problem you need to fix, you will not find a solution through complaint. Opening yourself up to a more creative approach makes you a better problem-solver, and you will probably resolve what's bugging you so that you'll have nothing to complain about.

Creators do:

Seek meaning in every experience.

Act with self-compassion.

Appreciate their humanness before taking the next appropriate action.

Take accountability for their choices and all that comes into their lives.

Engage in life knowing that both the smooth and the bumpy experiences hold possibility for insight and growth—and even a bit of fun.

Acknowledge their frustrations or disappointments, the things that aren't working as well as they would like—and then work like a dog to create positive changes.

Feel good. Creators recognize that life is dynamic and fluid. They roll with uncertainty, because they know that any change means growth and expansion, and the troubles are bound to be short-lived anyhow.

Creators do not:

Blame others for their unhappiness.

Focus on what isn't working.

Beat themselves up when they make a mistake or fall into a funk.

Make excuses.

Wish things were different. Creators work with what is.

So where do you fall on this spectrum? Are you a creator or a complainer? If you'd rather move into the creator category and toward your goals instead of being stuck in the same old routine, begin by consciously adding a couple of the things that creators do into your life and eliminating a habit or two from the creators do not section.

You'll change the moment for the better. But fair warning: Living life as a creator is not for the complacent. It's full-contact living.

....

PERENNIAL PRACTICE: TRANSFORM THE COMPLAINT

Write down three things you have a tendency to complain about. If you're like me, you probably only have a few things that really bother you, but you complain about them over and over and over.

Now, journal for three minutes about the ways in which you contribute to keeping these negative situations alive. What is your responsibility for this complaint? Perhaps you have unreasonable expectations; maybe there is a little sabotage going on; maybe you are simply in the habit of complaining, or you feel like you are not entitled to the good stuff. Perhaps you make excuses or blame others, so you are stuck instead of making the necessary changes.

Now write down one thing that each of these complaint-worthy items has taught you.

One of my pet peeves is disorder. I like to have an organized environment. When my husband comes home and dumps his change, earbuds, three days' worth of lunch containers, keys, glasses case, name badge, and whatever else is in his pockets or bags onto my kitchen counter, it makes me crazy. It's become a daily complaint of mine. It's become my focus, and I'm pretty sure my behavior has intensified my bad feelings about this not-so-big-of-a-deal thing and contributed to a certain negativity around here—some nights more than others.

When I did this exercise, I realized that the mess has taught me a lot about myself. It's showed me that I get too caught up in meaningless things. It's taught me about patience and tolerance and letting go. It's taught me that if it is that important for me to have the counter clean, I can do it myself.

Some days I'm good at doing all this, at letting it go, and other days not so much, but it's been freeing to know that I can choose to create a new experience from the same old complaint anytime I want.

....

Be Awesome: *Make today imperfect. Color outside the lines, make mistakes with wild abandon, try the things that hold risk of failure. Then tell somebody about your failures—about the things you messed up, or the flaw you hope no one notices. By learning to be comfortable with imperfection, we also become accountable, and we are able to become the creators of our lives. Notice too how all* *those errors you made led you to knowledge you wouldn't have otherwise had. This is awesome.*

....

YOUR PARTICIPATION IS REQUIRED

I used to hate Red Rover. You know, that game played in elementary school P.E. where the whiny kids on the other side chant: "Red Rover, Red Rover send Polly-or-some-other-weakling-who-will-never-make-it-back-alive right over."

I was little and wimpy and ran about as fast as some people walk. Yet every time they called my name, I believed in my heart of hearts that I would break through the human barrier. Every time they called my name, which was always first (in this game it's not a good thing to be called first), I silenced the butterflies in my belly and got my little legs churning. Don't think I ever made it through. Usually I fell down, or bounced off the clutched hands. My ego and body were bruised. Yes, it's all coming back to me now, and I'm feeling a little sick. But the point is, still I played—mostly because the teacher made me—but even then, I did my best. I was in the game.

I grew up with juvenile rheumatoid arthritis. It made it hard to walk many days, and sometimes it was excruciating to sit hunched over a school desk or sit crisscross-applesauce during show and tell. Often, I couldn't cross my legs at all due to swelling and stiffness. Many, many times it would have been physically easier to stand off to the side, to pull back, to make an excuse not to participate in school, in Red Rover, in anything.

But I never wanted to miss out, either. I couldn't do everything the same as the other kids. I wasn't very good at most of the physical stuff, à la Red Rover, but I wanted the experience of being in the game. Wanted to try. To be a part. To participate.

That's where the life is—in our participation. It's not in the winning or busting through. It's in the way we smell the flowers and skip to the bus with our seven-year-old and taste the chocolate cake. It's in how we love and how we deal with failure and how we grieve. It's in how we manage stress when the bills have arrived but the paycheck hasn't.

Life isn't a spectator sport. To really live, we've got to push in and allow ourselves to be surrounded by the challenge and beauty and stress and opportunity. To slow down long enough to feel the emotion—all of it—even when it is opening us up or pushing hard against our hearts.

....

IN THE MOMENT PRACTICE: REMEMBERING TO EXPLORE

Take five minutes and reflect on a time when you badly wanted to do something you were afraid to do. Maybe you were a child wanting to try the new roller coaster, or a college student wanting to ask a woman out on a date. Maybe you wanted to move to a new neighborhood.

Remember the anxiety and fear you felt contemplating this scary but exhilarating thing. Then remember how you felt about what happened next. If you pursued this thing, how did it feel when you got it, or lost it? If you stayed on the same path without going after the thing you thought you wanted most, what did that feel like? There are no wrong answers.

Life is full of fits and starts. But to live an awesome life is to be in the process of discovery and exploration. We all have moments where we didn't go after what we wanted. And we all remember times when we did, despite our fear. Those moments, when we pushed through our fear—no matter the outcome—are the ones that usually give us the greatest satisfaction. Maybe we failed, but at least we gave it a go. That's what it means to be engaged.

....

Power Up: It is sometimes scary to do new things in life. To do the things that matter. To participate fully. But consider this: It is much scarier, and much less rewarding, to live an entire life on the sidelines.

You don't have to change who you are to be awesome; you just have to step up and in and be all of who you are. To recognize your imperfections, to own your talents, to love openly, to cry when you feel like it, no matter where you are. To show up. Be present. Engage.

This is risky, right? It feels scary. Vulnerable. Seriously, I'm suggesting you cry if you feel like it—in public? I'm saying you could tell others you love them? I'm suggesting you get off the wall and play Red Rover even though you're going to fail repeatedly (clearly, I'm not over it yet), even though you're never gonna break through the chain? Yep. Yes. Get in the game. Even if you lose, get your heart stomped on, your ego bruised; it's still worth playing.

THE RISK OF NOT PARTICIPATING

We often associate risk with a threat to our physical body—cliff diving equals risk—or a threat to our finances, à la investing in the stock market.

But the scariest thing of all is the idea of getting to the end of our days here on this planet without having done anything of significance. Even as a kid, I knew that my future success wasn't dependent on how well I played Red Rover, thank God. I felt embarrassed, sure, that I was such a terrible Rover. I felt awkward, like I didn't fit in at times, but I knew the future held more for me than playground games.

Fast forward to starting a business when I didn't have a dime in the bank; getting married; having a kid; writing my first book— that is downright scary stuff. These were the things that felt risky and uncertain, because they mattered so much. To fail at any one of these things would have meant heartache, and financial hardship, and a lot of discomfort. It would also mean I'd need to reevaluate who I was. Or at least who I thought myself to be. Almost seemed safer not to try.

Yet the thought of *not* sharing myself in a relationship, or *not* writing the book, felt scary too—and not having the courage to try, downright depressing.

Economics professors and psychologists talk in terms of risk and reward. There is always risk in participating, says Brené Brown, researcher at the University of Houston and the author of *Daring Greatly.* We avoid, deny, and hide to stay safe. But that's not engagement. That's not participating.

If you fail to dare, if you decide that going after the awesome in your life is too great of a risk, then you will stay put. It might be comfortable, easy, familiar for a while. You know the routine. It isn't all that bad. But it can never be bigger than that. It won't ever be better than "not bad," and in the end, that's not enough. Is it?

When you take the risk to live fully and wholly, to try new things, to go after what matters, to explore your passions and purposes, you are exposed—physically, emotionally, spiritually. Mostly spiritually. Sure, this is scary. We are wide open, and from that position, anything can happen. But that also means *anything* can happen. The possibilities are unlimited.

This is the awesome, you see? Because when we are afraid to risk our comfort and familiarity, we run the greater risk of living a narrow, bland existence. When we put ourselves out there, we access the awesome that is already within us and the awesome that surrounds us.

I'm not suggesting you sell the house, pack up the kids, and move to Tahiti. But you could. To participate in life, you don't have to climb mountains, or invest all your moolah in the Next Big Thing, or get divorced and become a cougar—though if that's where your passions lie, I guess that's your deal.

What I am suggesting is that you decide to do the things that matter to you, and put all your *oomph* into them. Some of the greatest risks I've taken in life have occurred right here in my three-bedroom ranch house. I risked professional failure and wrote a couple of books. I risked personal pain when I got married and poured my life into a child. I risked public embarrassment when I downloaded Helen Reddy's *I Am Woman* onto my iPod. And all of these things have made for an awesome life. The risk, my friends, is not in what you do; it's in the not doing.

THE COURAGE TO PLAY

Now, don't go all crazy on me. I'm not suggesting you leap off the high dive on the first day of swimming lessons. You can wade into the water, get clear about what you want, and mitigate the risk by learning what you need to know. You can prepare and train and practice and have fun in the process.

I experienced this last year when I enrolled in a beginning ukulele class. Talk about scary. I am so not kidding. But when I was given the ukulele as a gift, I knew I needed to play it. I wanted to play it. I wanted to participate. And I was petrified.

So, I worked on it a bit. At home. Alone. Behind a closed door. Believe me, this was best for everybody.

Cynthia Pury, professor of psychology at Clemson University, and other researchers say that courage is something that can be developed. One of the ways to do that, Pury says, is to prepare and practice ahead of time. Do what you can to gear up for the action you are about to take and remember why you are doing it. When you are clear about your goal and you work to minimize the risk by preparing and practicing, your courage grows.

Here's how it works. I am freaked about publically playing the ukulele, but my goal as part of living an engaged life is to continue learning and growing. To try new things and open myself up to new experiences. So instead of waiting for ukulele class, I bought a beginner's book and started strumming away on my own. I became familiar with how to hold the little thing and where to line up my fingers. I even learned some of the terminology, like *frets* and *neck*. By the time I signed up for a class, I was still totally nervous, but at least I knew how to hold the sucker. That gave me some confidence. So, was I good? Nope. But I did have fun. And I felt braver and stronger for having tried.

Fear, risk, courage—they are different for all of us. What is risky to me may not faze you one bit. The important thing is to be willing to risk your comfort to live a big life, one that is satisfying, engaging and awesome.

HOW TO LIVE AN ENGAGED LIFE

Socrates once said, "An unexamined life is not worth living." I agree, plus I like to name-drop by quoting Greek philosophers like Socrates. But I think he was on to something when he stated that an experience isn't meaningful unless we contemplate it, explore it, feel it, and reason through it. We cannot engage in this life if we don't notice what we are doing.

Here are five ways to start noticing:

Show up. Be willing to be present. If you want to criticize a public policy in a letter to the editor, fine, but sign your name. Are you urging your buddy to apply for the promotion? Good, but be prepared to take a step toward your own greatest goal at the same time. Want to offer tips to your kid about how to do better in school, or in soccer, or at making her bed? Then be willing to listen when she has suggestions for you. Be willing to share your shortcomings and failures while you continue to learn new things. Stop talking and start doing.

Cultivate curiosity. Curiosity not only makes life more interesting and awe-filled, but it also prompts novelty, builds meaning, and contributes to well-being, according to scholars Todd Kashdan and Michael Steger.

Curious people also say they are more satisfied with life. When our curiosity is piqued, we get involved. Often we are inspired to learn more, to understand our lives in a new context. Sometimes this leads to big changes and contributions, like for the little boy named Albert Einstein, who was fascinated by the workings of his father's compass and was compelled to learn more about electromagnetism. That worked out.

Curiosity drives us to explore life, and that leads to unique and repeated experiences which develop our brains by creating new neural pathways. Our experience expands, our brains grow, we feel more satisfied, and all of that makes us healthier, according to research by health psychologist Gary Swan.

Choose wonder over worry. Wonder, much like curiosity, prompts exploration and contemplation. It requires us to participate, to contemplate, think, reason, explore, try. Worry just freaks us out. It keeps us sitting on the couch, obsessing over the same thoughts that ultimately come down to how we aren't good enough, or he's not good enough, or life isn't fair. Instead of stepping into life, we step back and stay stuck while eating the mound of mini candy bars (pretty sure four minis equal one full-size bar) that the kid brought home from the school Halloween party.

Worry looks like this: *OMG, what will the neighbors think when they see the wine bottles from the last two months in this week's recycling bin? I shouldn't have put them out there. Why, oh why did I do that?*

Wonder looks like this: *Huh. I wonder what else I need to be recycling to help create a more sustainable environment?* Or, *I wonder if I have more wine bottles in here than anyone else on the block?* Or, *I wonder whose bin I can toss my bottles into?*

Wonder gets you thinking, trying, playing, moving. Worry just leaves you trapped.

....

IN THE MOMENT PRACTICE: CHOOSE WONDER OVER WORRY

Consider something that has you worried. Money, weight, kids, relationships, health, when you'll have time to shop for groceries, what you'll wear to the corporate cocktail party. Whatever. Get it in mind. Now ask yourself these three questions:

1. *I wonder why this has me so concerned?*
2. *I wonder what I can do to stop obsessing and feel a little better?*
3. *What is the lesson in this; how can I use this situation to grow?*

Feel better? Often all it takes to move from worry to wonder is a few good questions. When we start to question and explore our experience of worry, the emotional intensity diminishes and we get caught up in the curiosity, which is active and fluid rather than stagnant and stuck.

....

Allow your emotions. Emotions can be a source of insight that help us know ourselves better. They show us what is working and what isn't. When you feel icky, it's probably because you're not on track. When you feel love, or excitement, or curiosity, or joy, it's because you are in alignment with your desires and passions and authenticity. Instead of suppressing the hard emotions, use them. Notice what they are telling you and use them for motivation.

Be brave and accountable. All this life engagement is good when things are comfortable and fun, but be present too when things are tough. Do what you say you are going to do and work with the consequences that come from those actions instead of blaming or making excuses or resisting. When the game-winning shot comes up short, when you do something that disappoints your loved ones, when you don't get the promotion everyone thought was yours, stay present to those moments too. Sometimes full-contact living hurts, but those setbacks provide the contrast we need to fully live in the moments of awesome that are also there.

ENGAGING THROUGH COMPASSION AND KINDNESS

Often the best way to engage in experience is to lead with your heart and with the energies of compassion, love, and kindness.

Some of the most awesome experiences in our lives come when we connect with others, and especially when we allow them to touch us. Think about a first kiss, or seeing a birth, or walking down the aisle, or watching your child graduate. Think about moving into your first house, or buying your first car. Or remember hiking over a ridge at sunset, or taking that first, perfect sip of morning coffee. Moments like these shape a life. And while we each have our own take on the world and a unique experience within it, this stuff is also universal.

We approach our lives with our own original flair, but we come together as part of this human collective. That means that we all experience loss and joy, fear and disappointment. We have all been there. And for that reason alone, everyone is worthy of our kindness and compassion.

When you can, take a moment to connect to someone's pain, or smile even when they've treated you poorly. If you can reach out with empathy and understanding instead of berating them for bad behavior, you are engaging in life at the fullest level. In those moments, you can remind us all about how awesome it is to be human.

....

Do Good: *Today, engage in a random act of kindness. Do something for a stranger; leave chocolates for a friend; buy lunch for the couple at the table next to you; help a senior load the groceries into her car; write a letter to someone you love, telling him why.*

....

It's not always easy. Sometimes I'm feeling so wound up and PO'd that I'm not thinking about being nice. When we engage with others in a hostile and angry way, the hostility and anger only heighten. We move into a tunnel of stress where it becomes harder to breathe, harder to participate, harder to be a creator in our lives. We feel off-center and bad about ourselves, and that carries over into impatience and anger at others. We become blaming. Pouty. Closed.

But when we meet someone with compassion, when we act with kindness even if they've acted poorly, the opposite happens. We feel uplifted. More peaceful. Attuned to compassion throughout our lives. We may still not feel good about the initial action, but the hostility is muted and replaced by understanding. This allows us to move up and on. Compassion yields gratitude, appreciation, and awe.

How you move through the world is totally up to you. Whether you lead with compassion or harshness when wronged is a choice. I'm not judging, because I've done it both ways. But compassion has always been the better choice.

Nobody has to earn it. Everyone is worthy. Compassion is a gift you give, or not. You don't owe anyone. When something goes haywire, you can always assume they are out to screw you and they aren't good people anyway, those jerks. And you may be totally right.

Or you can live in a world where the potential for awe is everywhere—even in the guy who just cut you off on the freeway. You can remember that everyone hurts, everyone loves, and everyone makes huge, massive, jerky mistakes, and you can connect for just a second during those moments with a little compassion. You can take a second to imagine what his experience may be like; to remember that he might be afraid or insecure or stressed out too. Just like you have been once or twice. And you can be a little more patient, a little more loving, a little less reactive. You can let others have their own experience and move away from it if it hurts or feels bad, but you can move away without doing harm.

You want to live an awesome life? To live up to your potential? To feel good when you wake up in the morning? Compassion and kindness are the quickest ways to get there, and at their essence, they are the deepest way to engage in this life. They are also part of our authentic nature.

....

Night Cap: *When we recall being treated with kindness and compassion, we are inspired to act with kindness toward others. Try it: Think of a time when somebody treated you with surprising kindness or compassion. What did that person do? What did the moment mean? How did it change you going forward?*

....

CHAPTER 3:

GETTING REAL

■ ■ ■

I know of nothing more valuable, when it comes to the all-important virtue of authenticity, than simply being who you are.

—CHARLES R. SWINDOLL

Early in my career, I worked in public relations. I wore suits. I had business lunches at places with fabric napkins and lots of silverware. I sat at tables with some of the city's top executives and smiled and used big words. My secondhand Honda with the dent in the bumper was often parked in the lot next to Mercedes and BMWs. And I was making some money. Living the dream—only it wasn't my dream.

I worked hard, but I wasn't all that good at it. I felt drained at the end of the day and often out of balance, out of sync, frustrated. I didn't fit in. What I was feeling, knowing, thinking, and desiring weren't congruent with what I was doing.

You can live a whole life like that—on the fringe, doing the thing that looks good on paper or in your bank account but never really feels right. Or you can be true to yourself and feel life open up.

To live truthfully, to behave in a way that aligns with what is going on within, is scary, energizing, and liberating. Anything else just keeps us stuck.

....

Be Awesome: *Access awesome right now by writing down one dream you've always wanted to pursue—writing a book; running a marathon; going to Hawaii.*

Now, take one baby step toward that thing. Behave outwardly in a way that will move you closer to the thing you hold in your heart, and awesome and inspiration will show up.

....

I once heard Oprah say that when she started her talk show, it felt so natural, it was almost as though she were breathing—that authentic, that real. And that is just plain awesome.

PEACE SETTLES IN

It's heart-rattling to wake up in the morning (assuming I'd slept) with a car payment and a house payment and no money coming in—but that's what I did for months when I resigned from my PR job to write full time. With my rate of savings at the time—thirty-eight bucks a month—it would have taken roughly a hundred years to save the amount recommended by the Small Business Administration volunteer who wisely coached me to wait until I had some money in the bank before, you know, quitting my job. But after waiting a year, the thought of staying in a place that felt so incongruent with who I was felt scarier still. So I resigned. I felt sick to my stomach, bit my nails, ate a lot of chips, drank even more coffee. At first. But soon a kind of peace also settled around the nooks and crannies of the fear. Despite the stress, chasing this goal soon felt more comfortable, inspiring, true than staying in PR. When I recognized that, I got fired up and excited.

An authentic life, one where you live the things that matter to you, isn't safe or easy or even comfortable—not always. Living close to your true nature requires you to stand in your authenticity even when it's unpopular or inconvenient, and sometimes even when it doesn't seem to make sense. You've got to be vulnerable. In the end, though, living an authentic life is always worthwhile.

Power Up: Living an authentic life doesn't mean that each moment becomes easy and comfortable. It isn't a guarantee that everyone will like what you bring, or that every job will be successful. But there is a peace and freedom that come from knowing yourself and staying true to that. There is a vitality that comes when we are doing the things that matter to us. Decisions get easier. Relationships take on a new fortitude and we become more resilient.

WHAT DOES IT MEAN TO LIVE AN AUTHENTIC LIFE?

Think cheese. Yep. Imagine yourself foraging in the fridge for a piece of cheese. You can get by on the processed stuff. It even works really well in some recipes. Flavor? Not bad. But it's not like gnawing on a hunk of aged cheddar. With the real stuff, the color is brighter, the flavor bolder, the texture firm all the way through. You may not like the taste of it. Cheddar cheese may not be your thing, but a sharp cheddar will always be distinctive and solid. What you see is what you get.

It's likely you'll never, ever find another analogy involving cheddar cheese in a personal development book, but I think authenticity works like cheddar.

To be genuine and authentic is to merge who you are—the characteristics, qualities, values, skills, flaws, and passions you hold within—with how you behave. What you hold within is reflected in how you move through the world. It is all of you.

In one of the first studies done on the subject, psychologists Brian Goldman and Michael Kernis defined authenticity as "the unimpeded operation of one's true or core self in one's daily enterprise."

In other words, you behave in alignment with who you know yourself to be: your values, your spirit, your core self.

So if the cheese looks like cheddar and smells like cheddar, we're counting on it tasting like cheddar when we take a bite. Thing is, many of us cheddar folks are living like the processed stuff.

LIVING OUT OF ALIGNMENT

On the surface, it may feel easier and more comfortable to keep quiet, play the part, go along, follow the rules—even when you don't agree. More convenient to simply nod your head or ignore or deny or suppress. Less troublesome. Right? We learn this often as children: Don't be too noisy, don't throw a fit, don't share your feelings, because that could be uncomfortable and boy, we wouldn't want that. If you are quirky or different or unique—and come on, we all are—it's best to keep it to yourself; otherwise others will make fun of you or you'll be disruptive in class. And please don't get caught making a mistake or taking a big risk and failing. That would be so embarrassing.

We learn to stay guarded. Take the responsible job, rather than the one we've always wanted to do. We tamp down our excitement, quiet our love (I mean, how awful to share your love with someone who crushes your heart), suppress our needs because we want to fit in and we don't want to feel bad. So we choose a role that provides social comfort and good manners over vitality and aliveness and connectedness.

This is like always wearing a lacy dress, when you are a jeans-and-T-shirt kind of gal. You'll get lots of compliments; after all, you look good in a dress—you can pull it off. But you are never quite comfortable, and you don't swing on the monkey bars or hike the nature trails, because your shoes hurt and your underpants might show. And so you miss out on things that would have been fun and felt good. Because you are uneasy wearing your dress, you are more focused on getting by without a major embarrassment than on creating an awesome experience. When we are living out of alignment, we go through life careful and cautious, rather than alive and awesome.

Maybe you stay in the job you hate for thirty years because it provides a stable income and Dad said that's what is important. You maintain a boring relationship because you are too afraid to share the depth of what you are feeling. Or you stay in the closet because it's too scary not to.

And you think, *What if I had done that thing I always wanted to do?*

When you are out of alignment, you feel a disconnect. That unsettling, sometimes downright icky feeling that comes when you are living someone else's life.

We've all felt it. We've all been cheesed. We've all had a moment where we nodded our head, went along, said nothing, did the opposite of what we knew was right while inside we were roiling with discomfort. It doesn't feel good to live an inauthentic life. Never. Ever.

FINDING YOUR VOICE

Here's how it works: When I wrote my first book, *Imperfect Spirituality*, my initial draft of the first three chapters was completely different from what was ultimately published.

At first, I wanted to be impressive. I wanted to be the expert. I thought I needed to be the smarty-pants authority in order to reach people. So I wrote the beginning of the book like that. Like some bigwig expert with an austere persona and a deep, echoing professor voice.

Thing is, I'm not all that impressive. I wear sweats and my voice isn't booming. I don't sling around a lot of big words—probably because I don't know a whole lot of them. I fuss at my husband. I love sandwiches and I am good with the remote, but I screw stuff up nearly all the time and I rarely look good doing it. That is who I am.

That doesn't diminish my passion for this material or my belief that it matters. I study and talk to the bigwigs and read the journals. I practice and live by what I write—until I don't. Mostly, I'm just doing my best to be kind and to live a happy and awesome life. Some days, I'm successful at it. Some days, I'm a mess. To act any other way would be inauthentic, and that just doesn't feel good.

So, when I wrote as the fancy-schmanzy expert in the beginning of the book, it was hard going. Those early chapters were a slog. I just couldn't get them right. Finally, I understood why, and when I went back to rewrite them using *my* real and authentic voice, the work got easier. It became more fun. It certainly was more meaningful. Some days I was even in flow. I felt vulnerable, for sure, because to write authentically also required me to share more of myself—the good and the rotten—but it also felt exciting and real and honest. In the end, it's boosted my confidence too, because when I meet readers, I feel like I don't have to be any different from what I shared in the book. It's who I am.

....

IN THE MOMENT PRACTICE: GETTING REAL

Pull out a pen and scrap paper and answer this question: What is one thing you don't like about yourself that nobody knows about yet?

Now, answer this: Why? What is so bad or terrible or embarrassing that you've got to hide it away? I'm not saying to go blurt it out, either. I'm just saying it's worth exploring.

Often, the thing we are most uncomfortable with is also the characteristic that makes us powerfully and sweetly human. The thing that binds us to others.

What truth does that one secret thing reveal about who you really are? When we deny aspects of our character, we often experience a sense of separation that makes it tough to act authentically. We put more energy into trying to hide and resist and deny those pieces. When you can identify those things you'd rather keep in the dark, you can work toward self-acceptance and compassion, and your genuine nature emerges.

....

WHOLE LIVING WITH BIG EMOTIONS, TALENTS, FLAWS, AND INSECURITIES

Today at breakfast my seven-year-old daughter, Sweet P (who now prefers to be called Pipps because she says *P* reminds her of pee and that's just gross), was negotiating a playdate. She wanted to invite a girl over who had never been to our house. She'd already talked to the kid, and things were a go as long as the mamas didn't get in their way.

"Do I know her?" I asked while spreading the peanut butter.

"You met her at the class party. She knows you're the mom with the big hair."

"The big hair?"

"Yes, all the kids know you're the mom with the big hair."

I'd like to say that next I ran my fingers through my long and lustrous full-bodied locks. And I tried. Oh, yes, I tried. But my fingers got stuck right there in the tangle, and when I pulled them through, I also pulled out several strands of the gray hair that were laced in the curls. Big hair? Big gray hair. There's no denying it.

Immediately, my daughter's comment triggered a bit of insecurity in me. All those times in school when I wanted to be one of the pretty girls with feathered hair. Imagine Little Orphan Annie with feathered hair and you see my problem. But to deflect or deny or even criticize my daughter for sharing this information would have been to deny an aspect of myself. It would have been to hide who I am, and a part of me that everyone can see anyhow. This realization came almost instantly, and so did the next: I like my crazy hair. The same hair that resembles a small shrub in the morning also suits me.

There are other aspects of myself that were harder for me to look at in the beginning. I'm not very patient, and sometimes not all that forgiving. I feel insecure when I don't feel heard. I'm anxious even when I know better. I'm afraid, too, at times. I can be very critical.

But it's only when we are able to recognize all of who we are that we can bring all those disparate pieces together into wholeness. When we can see to the core of our being, we learn that we are enough, right now, to cope with whatever comes.

"With self-awareness the hidden parts become known parts," says Susan Campbell (no relation, but awesome just the same), author of *Saying What's Real: 7 Keys to Authentic Communication and Relationship Success*. "We work to make the unconscious, conscious. Otherwise our problems and weaknesses are just projected onto others and that can even lead to war."

This kind of self-exploration can be pretty uncomfortable, though, because we've got to be willing to sit with difficult emotions. So here's a piece of advice: Just do it.

Feelings, Campbell says, are portals to knowledge and growth. To have any chance at authenticity, at true human connection, we must be willing to look at ourselves, big hair and all. When we do that, we develop the skills we need to navigate the complexities of this life.

THE BIG PAYOFF

Our ability to adapt and move with the changes and uncertainty that are a part of our daily life is dependent on our ability to live authentically. We cannot grow if we are unwilling to recognize our true nature. But when we realize that we are all of it—the good and the bad, the joy and the sorrow, the imperfections and the talents—in every moment, then we can bring that and use it to live an awesome life.

For example, it is possible to be afraid and still desire the very things you're afraid of. It is possible to feel love and loss. Human beings are complex systems, and like any system, we have many different moving parts and interests, Campbell says. To be genuine, then, we've got to get talking and working with all those parts.

"People who know all parts of themselves, those who become conscious, have more to bring to each moment," Campbell says. "Then you are all there, present, and feeling confident, no matter what shows up. This is the best thing you can do for yourself."

Power Up: When we embrace our true nature in our thoughts and behaviors, we are better able to move and grow with the uncertainties and changes in life. This boosts our resilience and helps us thrive despite challenge.

FINDING OUT WHO YOU ARE

To be genuine, then, you've got to invest some effort, because you have to learn who you really are. Authentic living is a big-time act of self-discovery. But much more important than the answers you'll find during this process of self-exploration are the questions you'll ask. It all starts with the questions.

So often, our sense of self is dependent on what others tell us or on how they act when we are around. Somebody says they like our hair; we decide this cut is awesome and we wear it for the next thirty years. A mother says, "I was never good at math either," and *boom*, all of a sudden her daughter can't pass the class.

But who are you without all those external forces shaping your sense of self?

....

PERENNIAL PRACTICE: THE BIG QUESTIONS

One of the reasons we live less-than-awesome lives is because we don't slow down long enough to get to know ourselves. The alone time we have, or the quiet time, is spent shopping, maybe, or watching our favorite show. If we're lucky, we get a massage or a manicure. But how often do you sit quietly and think about what you think? How much time do you spend exploring the feelings behind the behavior, evaluating whether you are living close to your values, and contemplating what you enjoy and what matters most?

Now is the time. Take thirty minutes to journal and answer these questions. When you take a little time to know who you are, then you are free to create a real and genuine life. And if you simply don't know, that's okay too, but don't let it drop. Get curious about the questions and the answers; commit to the act of self-discovery. An "I don't know" answer is simply an opening into self-actualization.

Who are you?

What are some of the labels you wear? (Mom, son, dentist, volunteer…)

Who are you without those labels?

Who would you be without your job? Your family? Your friends?

What do you value?

How do you demonstrate those values every day?

How do you fail to demonstrate those values?

What do you believe that is different from the beliefs you were handed as a child by your teachers, parents, and friends?

What do you know that is inconvenient, or different from what your loved ones believe?

When do you feel your best physically?

When do you feel afraid?

What do you wish others knew about you?

When do you most disappoint yourself?

When do you feel happiest, or most excited, or in flow?

Look over these answers, and continue to ask the questions. Don't judge. You will not be graded. There are no right or wrong answers here. In fact, the questions are always more important than the answers, because the act of questioning and contemplation allows you to know your authentic self. When you do, you are free to live from that place. Sure, it may be unpopular at times, but living from your higher, authentic self is always liberating and expansive and a whole lot less scary than living out some role others scripted for your life.

Now you can take deliberate action. Once you understand what makes you happy, for example, you can move toward that more often. When you know what makes you afraid, you are free to challenge and explore that fear and ask for help and support when you need it. When you know what you value, you can take action every day to behave in alignment with those values.

You see how this works? With knowledge and awareness, we get to take the steps that move us closer to our core, to the essence of who we are.

FIVE STEPS TO GET BACK TO YOUR TRUE NATURE

To feel good and comfortable in our skin, then, so that we are free to pursue our passion and purpose, we've got to live with personal integrity. We must behave in a way that supports what we say we value and hold dear.

This isn't all that hard when things are sweet. It works well, until somebody has a meltdown, or you can't find the taco seasoning because, ahem, the person who unloaded the groceries put it in the vegetable bin. It's all good until you've waited two hours in the oncologist's office and nobody even apologizes and you're scared out of your noggin and you try to meditate but instead you hyperventilate. Then the person you know yourself to be might also become a raving lunatic, shouting profanity while dripping with tears and apologizing all at the same time. Just sayin', could happen.

But you see, we are all of that too. Authenticity isn't always convenient or polished or even polite. Plenty of people aren't even going to like you for who you are. That's okay; you can love yourself through the less-than moments and use them to become more self-aware.

Here are some quick steps for coping when you are feeling authentically challenged:

1. **Pay attention to the emotion.** Feeling like going off on your husband over something he did or didn't do? Feeling insecure, sad, unsettled? Great! You've got something to work with. Now sit still. Just breathe and take a break from the activity around you. Become aware of your emotions and how they feel in your body.

2. **Observe your thoughts.** What's coming up? No right or wrong answers here; just notice. If your thoughts are saying "I need a glass of wine" or "He's a stupid-head," notice that and go a tad bit deeper.

3. **Press pause.** Alright, now, take a deep breath and take a break. You may need to say to your partner or child or friend, "Okay, I do want to work through this with you, but this has triggered something and I need a short break." A bit touchy-feely? Yep. Vulnerable, for sure. But so much better than wrecking the relationship, derailing intimacy and the opportunity for all things awesome because you were too afraid to be real.

4. **Stop the blame.** When you are blaming others, you are looking outside yourself for answers. Then you are no longer creating; you are complaining and staying caught up in the hurt and anger. Be quiet, then hold yourself accountable. People simply do what they do; there is no reason to blame yourself or anyone else. Identify and accept the situation. Consider your role in the mess. Then take action in keeping with your true nature.

5. **Start again.** Lead with compassion for yourself and others. Then stop fretting and complaining and whining and work on creating a new experience—one that matches up with who you know yourself to be. Keep going.

The payoff, when I do this stuff well, is greater peace and deeper relationships. Plus, I can live with myself a little easier because I haven't behaved like a total schmuck. I have always learned something.

But I don't always do it right. Sometimes I deal with my emotions by spewing and blaming and then feeling totally rotten about all the spewing and blaming. I am working on being more open and vulnerable and authentic even when challenged. This is my practice, and I'm taking it on wholeheartedly and teaching my daughter too.

Guess what? I've found it works anywhere at any time.

You may have to improvise a bit if you're at work, or the gym, or in line at the grocery store. You cannot always hit the pause button at work when your boss's controlling nature has triggered something in you, but you can go to the restroom and take deep breaths to understand what is coming up before you behave badly and get into real trouble.

I've taken a time-out with Sweet P too. When she inadvertently jabbed at my vulnerability as a parent, I was puffed up like a betta fish ready to do battle. But I felt the change in my body, caught my thoughts, and took a five-minute pause. When I came back, we had an honest discussion about our feelings without all of my emotional flares and irrational concerns that she would be sad and alone if she didn't have better table manners.

....

IN THE MOMENT PRACTICE: CREATE A SOUNDTRACK

I have Barry Manilow's "It's a Miracle" in my iPod, and if you'd asked me fifteen years ago, I would have denied it. But I like that song. It inspires me, and I'm okay if you mock me for my Manilow. I also have some Reba in there, and Patsy Cline, the Beatles, Katy Perry, Beyoncé, Adele, Steve Winwood, Jason Mraz, and Mozart, among others. I play them at different times, some while working out, others while cooking dinner or in the car. Although the songs are wildly different from one another, when I turn the music on, they fit the scene of my life just fine.

So, what is your soundtrack? Sit down and make a list of songs that express who you are—the fears and vulnerabilities, the passions and loves. The joy and anger and playful creativity that are you too.

What music fits you and why? This exercise will take you close to your true nature in all its dimensions and complexities.

Now, round up the music and put it together. Play it to keep you honest and close to your core self. It will remind you who you are: a multi-layered, multi-dimensional, awesome being.

....

GETTING COMFORTABLE

When you are acting in alignment with your core self, the clarity and freedom you experience will outweigh the vulnerability and fear. The fears and insecurities will still rise up at times, sure, but the fear is so much more suffocating when you are trying to live up to some unreal image and you're worried that people are going to find out you're a fraud. When you step fully into the moment with everything you've got, when you bring it, you will be free from that kind of crushing fear.

When you show your genuine self, when you are free to be all of that, then you are free to move into alignment with your talents. You will become more accepting of your imperfections because you know they are there to help you grow and learn. Authenticity, then, isn't some contrived image of who you'd like to be; it's a recognition of the person you are, and that is liberating.

"If you are hiding something from yourself, then your authenticity is just a veneer," Campbell says. "You've got to learn to live with your fears, instead of projecting those emotions onto another."

An awesome life is an authentic one. It's a more comfortable place to be because you can wear your pajamas to the bus stop, and say "no" when you must, and eat what you like and love whom you love. It's making mistakes. Apologizing. Forgiving. Trying again. It's freedom.

....

Night Cap: *When you turn off the light tonight, just before sleep, reflect on your day. When did you feel your best? What was your greatest success? When did you feel inadequate? Pause for a minute, and then think about one time when you were behaving authentically, in alignment with your core self. How did that feel? Consider, too, when you were acting out of alignment. Don't judge. Just notice the scenarios and situations that scare you back into inauthenticity.*

Often, our greatest successes, the things that are most personally satisfying, emerge when we are living from this place of wholeness. Notice how it shows up for you.

....

CHAPTER 4:

PUSHING YOUR POTENTIAL

■ ■ ■

*Ever since I was a child I have had this instinctive urge for
expansion and growth. To me, the function and duty of
a quality human being is the sincere and honest development of one's potential.*

—BRUCE LEE

In junior high, I was elected student body president. During the
election speech, I had to stand on the bench of the cafeteria table
to be seen. I was much smaller than the other kids. When the
votes came down, I remember thinking that things couldn't get
any better.

Good thing I was mistaken.

We all have moments like this when something special occurs,
when we leave it all out there. We do our best, and in return we are
rewarded with the thing we want the most. When we are young—
especially when we are young—it's hard to imagine things could
get any better. Then things tank, and in our despair, we feel as
though they couldn't get any worse.

When I was planning my wedding, many people told me it
would be the best day of my life. I was thirty-four years old, and

although some felt I was closer to living on a school bus with twenty-two cats than to marriage, I was fervently hoping that my wedding wasn't going to be my best day ever. I wanted a life filled with awesome moments, not just one biggie. I didn't want to peak at thirty-four.

The wedding was a great day filled with love and fun. I still get misty-eyed thinking about it more than a decade later. But in the years since that ceremony, I've had many other moments that have taken my breath away with their beauty and filled me with the kind of peace that only comes when you've done the thing you didn't think you could do. I've had moments when I let myself love in a stripped-open kind of vulnerable way and felt more alive than I had even the moment before.

I've eaten olives in Italy and rooted for my favorite team in the big game. I've held a baby—my baby—on my chest as she slept. I've heard the doctor say "benign" and had a dear friend call me when he arrived home safely from war. I've walked over the threshold of the house that we paid for—and are paying for still—with the money we are earning from careers that we've crafted. These have been great moments too, just like my wedding. And I know there is potential for more.

It's there for you too. You've got the same potential for great moments, great memories, great loves, great creations, great jobs, great successes. You've got potential for awesome abundance in every area of your life. You carry the potential for greatness within you. No matter where you go or what craziness is going on around you, you've got the potential, every day, to craft something awesome.

Potential means possibility. When you are living from a place of authenticity and you are less concerned with image and the ideas of others, you are expansive. Each experience, then, is a growth opportunity that drops you straight into a place of limitless possibility. It's within you if you are willing to push the boundaries of self.

Power Up: Potential is possibility. You carry it within, and therefore it is not limited by external factors. This means you can be awesome at any time, anywhere. You can craft greatness from any moment. This is your potential.

THE POTENTIAL OF ALL

When we talk about this kind of unlimited possibility, when we toss around that word, *potential,* it's often in reference to a brilliant young executive, or an athlete who has a shot to be the best. We talk about potential in terms of outward achievement. I think that is stifling.

You have the potential to write the book or run the race or invent the next thingamajig—and though some odds will be against you, you do have the ability to learn anything. You also have the potential to do things that interest you, to align with your values and desires, and to be happy. You can love deeply and live a meaningful life. Right now. This potential is there for you too. Yet those things often remain untapped. We feel like potential needs an external measure, a public result. But potential is personal. It is about your capability and courage to explore. Tolerate. Prevail.

We are capable of achieving more than we can even conceive. We can love big, laugh hard, learn, grow, survive, and thrive, and those things are ultimately the things that matter most.

Don't limit your potential to visions of external rewards— though that can be part of it. I like earning enough to buy a pizza and beer once in a while. But your potential goes beyond achievement. True potential is about becoming all of who you are. Authentic. Brave and willing to get close to big scary emotions. To take a shot at a relationship that stirs you. To bounce back after the hardest, scariest moments, and to thrive again. To have the courage to be a corporate manager, or an artist, or a mom, or all of it.

Potential is about possibility. It is about trying a new food you've never tried even though it's green and you don't eat green.

Potential is about how you engage in your life, whether you show up completely, not about what you're going to earn when you get there. When you make the most of every moment—even the painful ones—there will be plenty of internal and external rewards.

Reaching your potential, then, is a matter of reaching toward your own definition of success, says Robert Kaplan, Harvard Business School professor and author of *What You're Really Meant to Do.*

What I care about, what I'm passionate about, what I'm good at and terrible at and inspired by, are going to be different from what gets you going. Our potential can't be defined by others. No one else knows the energy and desire you've got stored up inside. Potential is a byproduct of self-awareness. Only you can know what you truly want to achieve. What you want the most may not be what your mom thinks you ought to be doing. It may not make sense or look good on paper. It may not be motivated by the bottom line. But it's only when you are clear about what you want to achieve, right now, that you will know where your potential lies—and then you can set off toward it.

If you are living deliberately, like those of us who are awakening to the awesome already in our lives, then potential is a hopeful quality. It is a beacon of light radiating through the fog of hard times, pointing us in the direction of our best selves and our greatest possibility. Potential reminds us what we are capable of.

Each success and every setback along the way will reveal a little bit more about who you are and help you to grow into who you are meant to be. Our capabilities are always beyond what we know them to be right now. But by exploring our inner landscape and engaging in the outer one, we can discover our own power.

THE NOW POTENTIAL

Deepak Chopra writes in *The Seven Spiritual Laws of Success,* "When we are in our essential state, we are pure consciousness. Pure consciousness is pure potentiality; it is the field of all possibilities and infinite creativity. Pure consciousness is our spiritual essence. Being infinite and unbounded, it is also pure joy. Other attributes of consciousness are pure knowledge, infinite silence, perfect balance, invincibility, simplicity, and bliss. This is our essential nature. Our essential nature is one of pure potentiality."

But, as with so much in our lives, it's not enough to have this potential. We must remember to access it; to pay attention to the possibility of our unlimited self.

You don't have to bother with thoughts about whether or not you are maximizing your potential—you are not. Our potential expands as we do. Yet, we may edge up against our potential in any given moment, think we've arrived. When we are living fully right now with all the skills and abilities we've acquired, this is the now potential. And it's pretty good. We feel as though we are at the top of our game, and we are, for a moment. But then what we are capable of, what is possible for us, expands into the next opportunity.

When we realize this, our self-awareness grows. So do our skills, knowledge, and courage, and that balloons our potential out around us in a bigger way. It illuminates what's available to us *now* and gives us a hint of what could be. In this way, the realm of potential and possibility inspires us to live fully as adaptive, creative creatures capable of anything. Now imagine what you can do when you believe that.

....

IN THE MOMENT PRACTICE: CONSIDER HOW AWESOME YOU ARE

Sit down. Turn off the phone. I mean it—Turn off the phone. For three minutes (set a timer so you don't keep looking at the clock—let's just say I know all the tricks), consider this question: What is the most you are capable of? What is the biggest, most stupendous, most amazing thing you are capable of? Is that it? Is that as good as it gets? How do you know? Sit with the question, and if

> *you cannot answer it, just know that there is plenty of*
> *awesome ahead.*
> ....

When it comes to creating an awesome life, to expanding into infinite possibility, there are no limits other than those we believe there to be.

KNOWING YOU CAN

The greatest way to access our potential for awesome, then, is to believe you can. To know you are capable.

Your beliefs about whether or not you can succeed at any task directly impact how you approach a goal and overcome challenges, and even determine the tasks you take on.

Psychologist Albert Bandura, who first coined the term *self-efficacy* in the late 1980s, found that when we believe we can do well, when we have confidence in our skills for a particular task, we are more likely to take on difficult tasks and persist.

The difference, then, between living an invigorating life close to your potential and staying stuck in something less than your best results from your beliefs.

BARRIERS TO PERSONAL POSSIBILITY

Beliefs are one of our biggest obstacles. When we are stuck and worried and grumbly, it's usually because we are caught up in how we think.

We sabotage ourselves and limit our access to all things awesome solely by what we believe. Beliefs are just thoughts that we've given special attention to. You know, the repeating thought patterns that begin when some teacher says you aren't good at math, or a parent says you're too fat, or you see a commercial that implies that Pepsi is the secret to youth and vitality.

We adopt these ideas like they are our own. We nourish them through our behavior. We believe we can't lose weight, so we think, *Why not eat the hot dog? It's not like I'm ever going to be thin anyway.* Or, *Why try for the promotion? Everyone knows I'm not the smartest one here.* Then, because of these ideas, mere fragments of our imagination, we act in a way that creates tangible results. We use those results as reasons to stay stuck in this place far from our potential.

We trap ourselves. But we can also free ourselves from that trap by examining what we are thinking and replacing the unhelpful beliefs with something better.

THREE STEPS TO REWIRING YOUR BELIEFS

1. **Identify the beliefs that are holding you back.** Look at the excuses you make and the fears you have. Why are you afraid to apply for the job, or go on the date? Look at the motivation behind your actions. When you notice what you are doing, you can identify and release the false beliefs that are driving the actions.

2. **Scrutinize your thoughts.** Some of your beliefs are there to serve you—for example, *It's better to love than to hate.* Others, like *I'm not worthy,* don't help a whole lot. Look at the thoughts that help and keep those. But the ones that hurt need further exploration. Question whether each thought is helpful, whether it makes you feel good, whether it helps you become a creator rather than a complainer. If not, let it go. Remember, beliefs are just ideas we assume to be true. Since we get to choose, why not pick only those that are helpful?

3. **Install a better belief.** When you're ready to clear out those beliefs that are not working for you, replace them with something else. For example, if you identify

that your beliefs about your weight or relationships are keeping you stuck, replace them with something that moves you toward the awesome you want to create.

I can never lose weight becomes *I am a person who makes healthy choices for my body.*

I am not worthy of a loving relationship becomes *I am a loving person; therefore, I'm worthy of love in my life.*

I'll never move ahead at work becomes *I am capable of learning what I need to know to create the opportunities I desire.*

Of course you are. You've got a body that blinks about sixteen times per minute to protect your eyes. A heart that pumps 1,900 gallons of blood every day to support an organism that is capable of inventing rocket ships and the Internet and the polio vaccine and the X-ray and doughnuts. Especially doughnuts. The galaxies are made of hydrogen and carbon and oxygen and other chemical components, and so are you. You are made up of the same stuff that forms the Universe.

You think you don't have the potential for a new job, or better health, or a big move, or a happy marriage? Pshaw. You got this. You are vast. Your capabilities are beyond what you even know. Stop worrying and start wondering about the awesome that comes next. This wondering moves you toward the outer edge of potential, and you'll keep moving from there.

Alright, so you got all this going on—unlimited possibility, pure potential, ability to leap buildings in a single bound—but how can you access your potential when the kid is out of underwear and you've got to thaw out the pipes with a hair dryer before the entire bathroom floods?

The question I have asked myself many times, not kidding, is "How can I maximize the possibilities in my life—the improved relationship, awesome job, bigger bank account, healthier body—when I can't even put an outfit together?"

Potential isn't just going to knock you upside the head and say

"Hey, this is your shot, now here's exactly what you need to do." It's going to show up in the way you problem-solve the disagreement with your husband and the connections you make while volunteering for the school carnival and the emotion you feel when you blow the deal. Each moment has the potential for awesome, but you've got to unlock it.

CRACKING INTO YOUR REALM OF POSSIBILITY

Potential is realized through learning and action. Learning what we love, identifying those things that make us feel successful, is a matter of adapting and of exploring life. When we explore, we take what we know and we try it out. We experiment. We test out our knowledge and our talents to see where success lies. We work at it. And we keep working at it to discover the intersection between our desires and our abilities.

This takes effort, of course. You may have the potential to act on stage, or run a Fortune 500 company, or raise five well-mannered kids without breaking a sweat—but you can't know that until you try. That takes effort and accountability.

Whatever you explore, experience, or achieve is all on you. Stuff is going to come crashing down, fly in your face, and set you back, and that's your deal. Your life, your experience, is your responsibility. While much is bound to happen that you have no control over, you always get to choose how you respond.

We hear this and freak out. *Too much responsibility. I'm so overwhelmed. Blah. Blah. Blah. Besides, it's not all* my *fault. Is it?*

But think of it this way: If you are accountable for your experience, you also get to reap the rewards for it. It belongs to you. Take responsibility for your mistakes and imperfections and you also get to own your success. That makes it more meaningful and more important. It puts you firmly in the place of a creator.

Don't do this in isolation. Seek out teachers and information. Explore, play. Take trips, get curious, do things that make you feel good. Persist even when things are hard, call for help when you need it, and surround yourself with people that are much smarter than you. But in the end, it's all on you. And when you can see the power in that, when you feel in your gut what a good thing that is, awesome is unlimited.

Power Up: When you are accountable for every aspect of your life—even your response to those things you cannot control—you become a creator, not a complainer. When you are a creator, the go-to guy, the one responsible for all the failures and imperfections, you also get to own your success. This moves you into your realm of potential.

So, then, make space physically and psychologically to explore this unlimited realm of your potential. Clear out some of the clutter. Be willing to wander out of the house, and your comfort zone, with an open mind. Create an open environment too, to dabble and experiment. If you want to explore your potential as an artist, clear a workspace and fill it with paints and supplies. Feeling the entrepreneurial spirit? Create an open window of time to begin researching your market. Clean out the rooms and cupboards and closets that are clogging up your physical space, and take care of the emotional clutter too. Release, surrender, forgive, let go of the worries and beliefs and painful memories that are keeping you from living your potential. Silence the background noises, resolve the distractions, and focus on all that you are, not all that you could have been. You are enough, right now, to do what you desire.

> **Live Well:** *Clean out a closet or the junk drawer or the bin under the bed. Pick one small, I-can-do-it-in-an-hour-but-I've-been-thinking-about-it-for-a-year task and get busy. You'll feel free, expansive, better when you're done. This will leave room for you to expand into other areas of your life.*

Here's how it works. You think you'd be good at managing a nonprofit organization that helps single mothers finish their degrees. You've got some skills—you've worked in management, have a business degree, and you keep your three-kid, two-cat household running smoothly. You get excited when you think of the prospect of really making a difference in the community.

But each day you've got the kids to feed and dress and get to school, and later, you'll be there to help with reading, and *then* you might drop by the dry cleaners and pick up your husband's shirts and stop by the gym on the way home before rushing back to meet the bus, make dinner, and coordinate bath time before bed.

It is unlikely that you'll discover your potential as the leader of a nonprofit if you're unable to push through the boundaries of the life you already know. You must mix up the regular routine and make room to explore your potential.

Make time for this. Skip the laundry one day, study your interests during a lunch break, have someone else run the errands so that you can begin to recognize your power.

This is a biggie. Potential isn't going to crown you, but the things you do along the way will reveal it. Make the time for self-awareness, for understanding how you define success and tapping into the talents that will get you there. Take steps to understand your strengths and weaknesses, your values, talents, and abilities. Then, pursue your potential from all sides. Do the thing you aren't sure you can do, and put larger possibilities into play.

....

PERENNIAL PRACTICE: DISCOVERING THE POSSIBILITIES OF YOUR POTENTIAL

Pull out your journal, We are about to begin exploring possibilities. Consider each of the following questions:

1. *Visualize a time when you blew the cover off the ball. You had everything working; you were at your absolute best and loving it. What was the situation? Where were you? What were you doing? What skills did that require? What challenges did you overcome? Spend a few minutes writing about this experience.*

2. *What are the strengths you have that contributed to that moment?*

   Go to the root. If you were good at organizing the family anniversary party, write down the individual skills you used to do that. If you brought a load of compassion and caring, how did that show up? Get clear on what you have going on.

3. *List the things you had to overcome, the things you weren't so good at. How did you deal with those challenges and still continue to maximize your capability in the moment?*

4. *Write down other situations where your strengths and interests could combine to help you max out the possibilities in your life. Just play here. No rules, just imagine the grandest possibilities that require what you have.*

5. *Now, keeping your unique skill set in mind, look for the opportunities—even the crazy, outlandish ones—*

that exist in your world that require your skills and ideas. What possibilities abound for you and the talents you offer? Make a list as you see them throughout the course of a week. At the end of the week, notice that there is no shortage of possibility for you to find your Now Potential.

....

Sometimes we think that what we've got isn't needed or relevant. Of course, this is hogwash. We need you to bring it—all of what you've got—because that creates possibility for the rest of us. Then we all get closer to the heartbeat of passion and purpose, to making good on our goals.

....

Night Cap: *Often, outsiders—parents, mentors, friends, coworkers, teachers—can help us identify our Now Potential. They can also get in the way of it.*

Reflect on the compliments you've received as well as the criticisms. Which ones jive with what you know about yourself? Which ones don't seem to fit? If someone sees your artwork and thinks it's awesome, and you are passionate about art, perhaps that is a direction worth exploring.

If your mom, however, suggests your analytical abilities are a good match for law school, but you hate suits and conflict and aren't too good at keeping track of details, you need to scrutinize your own strengths and abilities before deciding to enroll. Only you can know your potential. Only you can define success. It doesn't have to look like anyone else's. It doesn't have to match up to the expectations of others. Potential is personal. Use it to illuminate your awesome.

....

....

Be Awesome: *Today, remember a time when you did something you weren't very good at. For me, this is a matter of which one to pick. Let's say knitting. I am really, really not good at knitting. I've tried hard to knit. I've failed and tried again. I failed in a very public way in front of a friend's knitting group. And I learned to laugh at myself. By recognizing that I'm not a knitter, I've also been able to see other talents that I do have. Living awesome is about living whole and identifying both your imperfections and talents. When you see that you are capable of coping despite your flaws, you will know that you are all kinds of awesome.*

....

ONE PATH: CREATING AN AUTHENTIC LIFE

Amy Pearson was miserable.

On paper, her life looked glorious. Pearson, a policy analyst at a respected think tank, had a long list of successes. But she hated the life she was living.

"I was a performer, trying to be accepted and loved through achievement. I was chasing gold stars. On the outside I was sparkly; underneath, I was stuck and unhappy. Even though I was doing all the right things, I couldn't find happiness," she says.

Then Pearson's mother died unexpectedly. Three months later, her first children, twins, were born.

"Losing my mom was like a brick dropping on my head. And then my children were born. I'd tried to have children for six years, but raising kids wasn't anything I knew how to do, and it was then that I lost my ability to tolerate bullshit. I didn't care about mortgage reports or tax policy. I didn't want to read newspapers. All I wanted to do was read those self-help books."

Pearson laughs about it now, seven years later, but before, she says she was "too busy with her facade" to read things like self-help books or to do any of the other things she secretly desired.

After the death of her mother and the birth of her children, Pearson began reading all the self-help books she could find. Though she was exhausted from grief and caring for her newborn babies, a transformation was taking place.

It was then that Pearson stopped trying to be the perfect over-achiever and started connecting to what was true for her. She went after what her heart desired instead of what would garner the approval of others.

She left her job as a policy analyst, and while she was raising her kids (a third came a few years after the twins), Pearson also learned to be supportive of her own "crazy ideas." When she felt compelled by the work of author and coach Martha Beck to become a life coach, Pearson wholeheartedly pursued that path. She is now a master certified coach and trainer, helping others to overcome their own need for approval.

"Approval addiction keeps us from connecting to ourselves by basing everything on external approval. That is connected to why we are so unsatisfied in our lives," Pearson says.

When we move beyond this need for approval, this need to be all things to all people, it can feel scary and vulnerable for a while, Pearson says. But after that, it is liberating.

"The sense of deep intimacy and belonging that people need and want and try to cultivate through external approval is not possible when we live inauthentic lives," Pearson says.

But when we are authentic, we are connected and free to pursue our best lives, to challenge ourselves and pursue our passions and dreams.

"There is a feeling of relief that washes over you when you fully open to who you are," Pearson says. "I was definitely out of my comfort zone; even thinking about this was new, and I had no idea at that time how to coach—but I was also so strengthened by it."

We become stronger when we live from that authentic place, she adds.

Pearson has also learned to rely on the sensations in her body to help her stay on track toward the things that are authentic and important to her. She calls it her "body compass," and by paying attention to how she's feeling, she gets a sense of whether she's being true.

Living authentically just feels better, she says. And it's made her a more compassionate person.

"I've learned what it is to be truly kind," she says. "I'm not being kind anymore out of obligation or to get others to approve. Now it comes from a place of real kindness and real caring from my heart. I share more of myself and I speak my opinions more often. People don't always like it, but I'm okay with that and I'm not unkind."

CHAPTER 5:

GOING FOR IT

What you get by achieving your goals is not as important as what you become by achieving your goals.

—HENRY DAVID THOREAU

Sweet P has big plans. She wants to be a veterinarian with five cats and five dogs and maybe a bunny, and she wants to be a teacher and a mommy with two kids—that number has recently come down from seven. Her thinking isn't bad. Part of the reason she wants to have kids is, after all, so that they can help do the chores and clean up after the animals. But when I asked her why she chose all three of those roles, she didn't take long to think about it.

"I just want to help people," she said.

That there just might be the goal worth striving for.

Whether she will achieve these goals even after things like pooper scoopers, student loans, and diapers become part of the reality, it is too early to say. She's seven; we don't expect her to have her life mapped out until she's, well, at least eight and a half.

But going after such a meaningful goal might just help her craft a meaningful and satisfying life. One that is full of all kinds of awesome.

While a discussion of goal setting and achieving is so, well, '80s, research emerging in the last twenty years indicates that it's the quality and type of goal we set that determine the kind of life we'll lead, much more than any outcomes we achieve. The goals we choose from the get-go have a significant impact on how satisfied we are in life.

Power Up: The goals you choose are more important than the outcomes you receive when it comes to creating a satisfying life.

This isn't only about the pursuit of happiness, though happiness usually arrives when we engage in things that we care about. I'm talking about creating a whole life, one filled with meaning and well-being all of the time, not just during fleeting moments. Goals can be a way of helping us focus, or of rooting us as we explore what our purpose is. They are a structure by which we can see clearly whether we are on the right track or veering wildly off course toward a half-gallon of Chunky Monkey ice cream. Believe me, even the best goals do involve eating ice cream. But when we take care in choosing our goals, the process itself becomes a way to manifest well-being, good feelings, and all things awesome.

"A wise person," writes psychologist Robert Emmons, a specialist in the study of happiness and gratitude, "chooses fulfilling goals rather than those that offer the illusion of fulfillment."

CHOOSING THE RIGHT GOAL

Fulfillment, which is really a combination of satisfaction and meaning, doesn't generally show up via the Internet. Sure, that didn't stop me from doing a comprehensive search on Facebook, and while I did pick up some recipes and celebrity gossip, nary a hint of fulfillment was to be found.

Nor do meaning and satisfaction reside in money earned or

pounds lost or trips taken or other external rewards. Those things can provide in-the-moment gratification and muted satisfaction, and sometimes good feelings.

But when we choose goals that support a lifestyle we want to create, those that meet our needs of connection and belonging and align us with the values, issues, and relationships that matter most, our lives are permeated with sustained well-being and satisfaction.

THREE GOOD TYPES OF GOALS

In his research, Emmons has found that there are three types of goals that correspond to well-being, personal meaning, and positive emotion. He classifies them this way:

Intimacy—Goals that express a desire for close reciprocal relationships.
Spirituality—Goals that transcend self.
Generativity—Fancy term for goals that show concern for others and future generations.

Goals that fall into these categories might look like this:
"I will be a good listener."
"I strive to accept others as they are."
"I am working to make a positive contribution to the world."
"I want to be more compassionate and accepting of others."
"I want to be more supportive and patient with my family."
"I want to strengthen my spiritual practice and relationship with God."
These goals require us to show up, engage in life, connect with others, and get to know ourselves in a deeper way. That makes us feel good. Involved. Like part of the team.

I'm not saying our other aspirations to make a million dollars, become famous, run the marathon, or lose the weight aren't worthy, but the research indicates that they do not necessarily correlate to greater life satisfaction. They are not enough.

People with goals that focus on power or a desire to impress, influence, and impact others actually suffer more than those who choose goals that fall into the generativity category. Generativity goals involve creating, teaching, helping, parenting, or otherwise fostering behaviors that support connection.

In one study, the psychologists who developed the Self-Determination Theory of motivation, Richard Ryan and Edward Deci, found that those people who pursued more power-based achievements tended to focus primarily on external rewards and material gains as a means of happiness. Yet this outward focus makes it tough to create the social connectedness we crave. It is also harder to achieve these externally focused goals. We are more likely to attain goals after anticipating the internal rewards, rather than external payoffs.

....

Be Awesome: *Today, evaluate your values. Identify your top five and choose goals that support them. This is a path to awesome living. When our actions are inspired by the things we value, our lives take on a greater sense of purpose and meaning, and that creates a sustainable form of happiness called values-based happiness, according to the work of psychologist Steven Reiss. This happiness is not based on an event or acquisition, but arises from the satisfaction we feel when we are living in accordance with what matters.*

....

INTERNAL RESONANCE, EXTERNAL REWARD

This doesn't mean that you should eschew the money or the attention that comes from fulfilling a goal that also happens to improve the world or support your family or help you connect with others in a meaningful way. It simply means that you may not want to hang your goal on the external outcomes alone. If you are pursuing the right goal, the one that keeps you engaged and connected to the things you intrinsically value, you're more likely to persevere and overcome the obstacles that are bound to show up. Another thing happens too—the process, the day-to-day pursuit, becomes more valuable than the outcome.

Here's how it works. You set a goal to write a book. In the end, you want a book sitting there on your desk—and a bestseller wouldn't be bad, either. But as you map out your goal, you realize that what you most desire is the experience of writing a book that helps others. You want to learn and grow as a writer. You want to connect with others during research and create something that will inspire, entertain, and support others too.

Of course, you've also got bills to pay, so it is necessary that this book yield some financial reward, but it isn't what you are focused on. You are not attached to the sales figures or the profits.

When the book is published and you hear from readers who find value in its pages, that feels awesome. You are inspired to create more, to do more to get the book into the hands of others. Sales go up, and you also feel greater satisfaction. It's cyclical, and there are both intrinsic and external rewards along the way, but the satisfaction is lingering rather than fleeting because you have aligned with the aspects of that goal that provide meaning in your life.

It's worth putting the effort out, then, to create goals that support our emotional, spiritual, and physical well-being—all things that help us access our awesome. Once we determine what it is we most want—the deep-down stuff—and establish our greater goals, it's time to take action to make good on them.

The goals that will ultimately empower us to persevere are the ones that we believe we can ultimately accomplish. They also fulfill some intrinsic human need, says success and motivation researcher Heidi Grant Halvorson, associate director of the Motivation Science Center at the Columbia Business School.

The biggest and best goals usually fulfill these basic needs:

Belonging. The most satisfying pursuits fill our need to relate to other people. While I can spend long (and happy) hours alone, working and writing, ultimately, I do want others to read what I come up with. I want the work to have value, a positive and lasting impact. I want to change the world for the better. Bet you do too.

Competence. Whichever goal you pursue, you must feel that you can do it. That you can be effective, or can learn what you need to know along the way to achieve the outcome you desire. For me, then, with my arthritic, unathletic body, picking a goal to climb a mountain would be an exercise in frustration and probably lead to a whole lot of ugly crying, which naturally would undermine my happiness. Mountain climbing is not something I would be successful at. Pick goals that will challenge you, but also those you feel like you can accomplish.

Autonomy or authenticity. To me, this is a biggie. Whatever dream you dream, it must be something that feels authentic. Something that reflects you and your values. Something consistent with the things you care about. If these things don't line up, chances are you'll have a hard time achieving your goal, and it's unlikely you'll find much joy in it even if you do.

....

PERENNIAL PRACTICE: WRITING A GOOD GOAL

I want to live with greater awareness. Be more open and patient in my relationships. Oh, and I'd like to do work that makes a difference. These are a few of the goals I'm striving for, and simply pursuing them makes me feel good.

This isn't to say that you shouldn't set a goal to lose

weight or get a new job, but go deeper. Look at the motivations behind those things. Which intrinsic needs will they fulfill? How will they support your well-being and life satisfaction?

Write down one thing you desire or want to achieve in each of the following areas:

Relationships

Spiritual development

Emotional/Physical health

Then, for each, write down the intrinsic need that will be fulfilled as you pursue this desire. Perhaps you desire greater intimacy in your relationship, and the things you do to create that will also satisfy your need for belonging, love, and maybe even security and better health.

Now, write down the skills you have that will help you achieve that goal. Also list the things you can learn that will help you en route. Look at the list. See, you can do this.

Pick one of your categories and write a sentence stating your goal. Be clear, be specific, be positive—talk in terms of what you will do to achieve the goal, not what you won't.

Finally, in one sentence, describe how that goal aligns with your other values and things that are important to you.

Now, go do something in support of that goal.

....

Here's how it works. You want to drop twenty pounds. And although you would love a new wardrobe, you know the real reason you want to lose the weight is to be healthy and active and alive and present for your children. Losing the weight will help you connect and interact with them in a new, more engaged way. You will also live longer and have more time with them. Plus, it will set a good example by showing that you value your health. We've got the intimacy category going here, a little of the generativity too, and the need for belonging is met. This goal, you discover after exploring it at its deepest level, also aligns with your value of good health. You get specific and write something like this: "Each day I choose to eat five fruits or vegetables and get an hour of exercise." Note the positive language: You are not talking about what you won't do—*I won't eat junk food*—but instead you are keeping your focus solely on what you will achieve. Goals that promote positive outcomes rather than focusing on the negatives tend to be more achievable. Now go eat a carrot or an apple and take a baby step toward your goal of greater health.

GETTING AFTER IT

This is the awesome part: You know what you want, you understand why it matters, and now you're going after it. Woo hoo!

Of course, there will be obstacles and setbacks and downers along the way. But when you open up to the process, your striving becomes fun and puts you on course to run smack-dab into more awesome. Simply by going after something meaningful, you will cause other unexpected and life-changing things to come into play. You may meet inspiring people, travel, have surprisingly awesome experiences, get to know yourself better, or see things that open you up in a new way.

Go after something that is meaningful to you, and the realm of possibility expands. Life becomes bolder simply because you showed up to participate.

This is not about positive thinking. This is about positive action. Positive doing. It's where you tap into your deepest levels of awareness to choose a goal that aligns with your authentic nature and pushes you into the realm of potential and possibility. Then, you get going. Working, adapting, trying, failing, growing, learning, moving closer to your goal. The process is infused with inspiration and creativity, and no matter what comes out of this, whether you achieve your goal or not, the effort has been worthwhile.

GET RID OF THE THINGS HOLDING YOU BACK

In the beginning of this process, it's easy to throw yourself behind your goal. We get fired up and that momentum carries us forward—for a while. Until we get a little tired or a little unsure and we decide we must watch TV instead of working out, or we snap at our spouse because the whole compassionate intimacy thing is tough to do when he's being irritating and washing the whites with the reds.

Then we fall back into our old bad habits, those that sabotage our forward progress and dampen the good feelings. You know what I'm talking about. We go along just fine, taking care of business, feeling awesome, until we don't. That's when our goals are in jeopardy.

Living your dreams, owning your awesome, isn't only about picking something to pursue. You've got to keep pursuing. You've got to make sound decisions in the moment and cope with future uncertainties and stay on track and in alignment with your authentic self. This requires patience and personal integrity, dedication and perseverance. You've got to keep going even when you don't want to. And sometimes living your awesome also means giving things up. Many times, the most positive action we can take is to stop acting in ways that hold us back.

Power Up: As important as it is to identify the steps you need to take to move toward your dreams, it's equally important to quit the things that are keeping you from them. Stop the bad habits that are holding you back.

If you are working toward optimal health, stop wandering the chip aisle at the grocery store and *start* buying more produce. Want greater intimacy with your husband? Turn off the television, stop interrupting when he talks, quit mocking and start talking. See how this goes? Want to write a book? Stop logging onto social media. Just sayin'. It's maybe potentially possible that some people do that.

A little awareness can help you identify the times when you are slipping into the old patterns that do not support your goal. Then you can replace those habits with something that will move you in the direction you desire.

OBSTACLE BUSTERS

Bad habits aren't going to be the only thing slowing down your forward progress. Temptation, fatigue, uncertainty, beliefs, and external factors are a few of the other things that are probably going to rise up and slam the door to possibility in your face. This is all part of the deal, so you don't need to worry about adversity; just prepare to move through it. I'm not saying you'll love the setbacks. You won't be able to neatly work through everything with a glass of wine and a good laugh—yet those coping strategies are powerful in their own right.

The path through adversity is not always clear. Often it is infuriating, doubt-producing, exhausting, and frustrating—been there, done that. But there is nothing like the satisfaction and joy that come from knowing you kept at it, did your best, and, in the end, created something better than before. Here are a few obstacle-busting strategies that you can use to head off adversity and keep going even when you feel like crying in the closet. Tie your shoes and pull up your big-girl pants. Let's get after it.

Set an implementation intention

This is the missing link for many of us goal-minded people. We know what we want; we choose obtainable, meaningful, challenging, make-a-difference goals. We anticipate the obstacles and develop a plan for coping. But, we rarely make a plan to cope with obstacles and stay on track toward our goals.

People who do take that extra step and put an implementation intention in place are twice as likely to make good on their goals, according to research by Peter Gollwitzer at New York University.

Through if/then statements, an implementation intention sets out an advance plan for how you are going to respond to obstacles or other circumstances before they come up. It gives you a clear direction to follow during times of uncertainty or temptation, like when you want to tear into a fast food joint instead of making a salad at home.

Here's how to set your own implementation intention.

Create an "if" statement. This is the cue, the circumstance, the situation that triggers action. When and if this situation appears, your intention will kick in.

Create a "then" statement. This is the action. This is how you will respond when the "if" happens. It could involve a behavior, or a movement, or a thought strategy.

When creating the intention, be sure to get very specific. Identify the circumstances, the time, the actions. Write it down and look at it frequently. This also helps build awareness about the situations that serve your goals and those that detract from your efforts. Then you can streamline your efforts so that they support your desires.

If it is a Tuesday, then I will go to the gym after work.

If my proposal is rejected, I'll take the feedback, make changes and send it back out within the week.

If I receive my monthly paycheck, then I will save ten percent.

If I feel hungry while driving home from work, I will drink water and chew gum until I can get home to cook a healthy meal.

....

IN THE MOMENT PRACTICE:
CREATE AN IMPLEMENTATION INTENTION

Following the steps above, take five minutes and write your if/then statement. Identify the environmental cue that will prompt the "then" response. Be specific. Outline a plan. Write it on an index card and look at it throughout the day to remind yourself that you have

laid the groundwork to prevail despite temptation or
fatigue.
....

Mental contrasting

"Contrasting a desired future with present reality" can help us to pick better goals in the beginning and keep us working toward them until completion, says psychologist Gabriele Oettingen.

It works like this: When you consider where you want to go—the goal you want to achieve—and contrast it with your current experience—where you are now—and then realistically identify the obstacles you may encounter between here and there, you're less likely to be stymied by the struggles and more likely to persist until you overcome them.

Failure is often a result of pursuing the wrong goals. We get caught up in the expectations of others, or the anticipated riches or beneficial outcomes of our dreams, without ever evaluating the process, challenges, and obstacles we'll encounter along the way.

When we understand the pros and cons of the journey ahead, we can then wisely decide whether we have a shot at accomplishing the goal, or whether we care enough to bother. If the answer to either question is "No," we can pick a new goal, one that may inspire us more and help us prevail despite setbacks.

Mental contrasting helps you contemplate your achievement beforehand, while keeping you honest about the obstacles you'll face en route. And if you already have an expectation of success, mental contrasting is a motivation booster, Oettingen says.

That's good information to have. It keeps us from wasting time on things that won't bolster the meaning in our life. It's not a disgrace to give up on a goal when you fill in that space with something more appropriate, something that inspires and motivates you.

Focus on what you will do, not what you won't

Halvorson and other success researchers say it's super important to focus on what you *can* do, instead of what you must *not* do. It's more effective, Halvorson says, to replace bad habits with better ones. *I will go to bed at 9:00 p.m.* instead of *I won't stay up so late.*

A big part of persevering in the pursuit of our goals is our ability to keep on with the goal-supporting behaviors without yielding to temptation or distraction. Our ability to say "No" in the right way at the right time is critical. And those who use the word "don't" as opposed to "can't" tend to succeed almost twice as often, according to one study.

Say someone wants you to go out on Thursday at exactly the same time you were committed to writing up your business plan to move closer to your goal of self-employment. You could say "Sorry, I can't do that, I've got too much to do." Or you could go with "No, I don't want to do that when I have work scheduled."

Listen to the difference: *I can't eat the dessert because I'm on a diet* and *I don't eat dessert; I'm making healthy choices.*

The word *can't* just feels punishing. It sounds as though we are weak and limited and missing out. *Don't* is empowering. You are in charge, making decisions that will help you remain dedicated to your goal.

It is your choice as to how much awesome you'll let into your life. When you use the word *don't,* you are decisive and staying focused on your ultimate goal. This will help you stay on track.

Suggest success

Psychological scientists Maryanne Garry, Robert Michael, and Irving Kirsch studied the power of suggestion and discovered that deliberate suggestion can influence how well people remember things, how they respond to medical treatments, and even how they'll behave.

The reason, they say, is because of our "response expectancies." This means that the way we *anticipate* our response to a situation influences how we will actually respond. In other words, once you expect something to happen, your behaviors, thoughts, and reactions will actually contribute to making that expectation occur. When it comes to picking and persisting at a goal, you've got to expect that you are capable. Don't get behind a goal that you don't believe to be meaningful or possible. Even if the obstacles are major and daunting, can you believe that you are capable of learning what you need to know to prevail? I think you are. I'm suggesting we all are.

....

IN THE MOMENT PRACTICE: ANTICIPATE SUCCESS

Think about one of the goals you are pursuing and consider an obstacle you will face along the way. Anticipate how you'll handle that obstacle. Imagine yourself responding efficiently, capably, and successfully. After all, you are capable of responding well to any challenge.

....

When we have chosen our goals well and we are taking positive actions and successfully navigating the obstacles, life gets interesting. Things just seem to show up; the right people appear. There is lightness and curiosity and a sense that anything is possible. This is fun, and it should be, because goals can often be the track that leads us to our ultimate passion and purpose.

....

Night Cap: *Imagine you are at a banquet receiving an award. What kind of award would it be? What is the most meaningful, most touching thing someone could ever say about you? What do you want to be known for? Now come up with one thing you can do during your day tomorrow to move you closer to that.*

....

CHAPTER 6

LIVING WITH PASSION AND PURPOSE

■ ■ ■

The more intensely we feel about an idea or a goal, the more assuredly the idea, buried deep in our subconscious, will direct us along the path to its fulfillment.

—EARL NIGHTINGALE

I'm not into the party scene. I'm stressed by small talk and don't even want to walk into a room of people I don't know. But if I'm invited to discuss ideas and practices and strategies, things that will help us live happier lives, I'm all over it. I will stay for hours getting so fired up and intense that sometimes I don't even want to stop to breathe. An hour feels like fifteen minutes, and by the time I'm done, I've been changed by the experience. Uplifted. Inspired. I am passionate about discussing how we can get our awesome on.

A friend of mine is passionate about cooking. Another, home design. I know people who are so passionate about creating that they show up with paint on their shirt or a camera in their hands every time I see them. When my husband has time to putter in his shop, I know he's always going to be late coming in, because he gets caught up in his woodworking. He loses track of time by falling completely into the moment.

That's how it works, passion. It hits you over the head, pulls you in, and fills you with enthusiasm and exhilaration. It is the impetus for awesome.

BUZZING ABOUT PASSION

Passion has become a buzzword of sorts over the last ten years. Articles and talk shows and websites, including my own, talk about the importance of finding your passion and living your purpose. So we go looking, unless it's after eight o'clock on Friday night and we are just too darn tired. Other times, we get up all excited and go out to look, but we come back frightened because nothing showed up. We didn't find our passion. In fact, we don't even know what we like anymore.

We do know that we aren't all that in love with cleaning out the soccer duffel or wiping up crumbs or scouring the bath tub or writing the annual report for the boss who only remembers our name when something has gone wrong. We do know, too, that it's a bit shallow to declare our passion for things like, uh, cocktails, or romance novels, or office supplies (boy, how I love me some office supplies). I mean, passion should be bigger than that, right?

In these moments, between loads of laundry and bill paying and dinners with friends who come clean and showered and ready to discuss foreign films and fine wine, it feels like everyone in the world is lit up by passion—except for you. It's a lonely feeling to not know what drives you. To feel devoid of this big-time awesome energy that everyone else seems to have.

KNOW WHAT YOU ARE LOOKING FOR

Don't worry—you aren't empty of passion. Passion doesn't pick favorites. You haven't been left out. You've just forgotten. Passion isn't something you have to seek—it is not outside of you. It's something you have to uncover. It's the desire within you. You've got the fire; it's just a matter of remembering what sparks it.

Passion is enthusiasm for an activity. It is a zest for a particular experience, which usually contributes to a zest for life. It is getting swept up in something simply because you love it, because it challenges and inspires you.

When you find your passions and explore them, you're bound to feel inspired, enthused, energized, and engaged. Alive. Passion moves you. It is active energy that compels you to take action, to live bold, try new things, step into and through your fear. For me, it's a whole lot more practical than woo-woo—it's the keep-going-ness. The thing that adds color to a gray routine.

Power Up: If you are feeling stuck, bored, lazy, tired, if you have a hard time describing what's fun for you, you are working from a passion deficit. Don't worry; you've still got this energy. Now it's just time to chisel it out of the routine.

Passion is also a visceral reminder of what is working in our lives. It keeps us moving when we might otherwise feel down and depressed. Ever known someone who worked through the loss of a relationship by training for a marathon or traveling to an exotic locale? Ever dealt with a stressful diagnosis by throwing yourself into your work or a hobby like painting or pottery?

Passion keeps us working toward the things that matter. It fosters creativity, enhances problem-solving abilities, nurtures relationships, and contributes to greater health and well-being by lowering the stress that contributes to heart disease, depression, autoimmune dysfunction, high blood pressure, cancer, and just about everything else.

Psychologists, including Todd Kashdan of George Mason University, also link passion to other positive emotions. People who do the things they love tend to feel happier. Those who claim to have at least one passion also tend to experience greater confidence and a sense of mastery that helps them build resilience.

FINDING THE FIRE

These are good things, of course, but how do we get there from here, when we are mired in a predictable pattern of jobs and kids and chores and spaghetti Tuesdays? At first, it's a jolt, to realize we aren't all that passionate about anything anymore, that we've forgotten what we used to do for fun. It's disappointing to no longer know what makes us feel alive. So we start blaming.

We say, "I'd like to paint, but there's no time with the kids." Or, "I want to learn to cook, but my husband won't eat that fancy food." Or, "I'm too old, too broke, too tired to do that anymore."

You can stay here in this limiting cycle of blame, or, you can get busy. This is where it gets fun.

HAVING FUN

Fun? What's that? I don't have time for that kind of baloney. Right. I know. No time, no money, no energy equals no fun. But here's the thing: When you are engaged in something you truly enjoy, you are not drained by it; you are energized. You have more *oomph* behind the other things you must do in your day. This means you are more productive.

This is not an expensive or taxing prospect. Passion does not have to mean jumping out of planes (thank goodness) or skiing down the black diamond slope (whew). It does not mean you have to get in shape or make loads of money or dye your hair.

It's not contrived. It's more of an encounter, a merging of your interests, desires, talents, and time. So the first way to find your passion again is to do the things that interest you—read a book, try a new recipe, draw the picture, connect with friends. That's what I mean by fun. Go toward the things that make you feel good.

This isn't frivolous, no matter what you have decided a grown-up is supposed to act like. It is not a luxury even if, sadly, we learn around the age of seven that we shouldn't be too silly or imagina-

tive or playful because that is just not cool. Fun is not wasted time
or energy.

> **Power Up:** Passion is a merging of your interests, desires,
> talents, and time. To find your passion, then, start by
> looking for the things that inspire and move you. The things
> that are fun, or used to be fun. Start exploring them again
> and see what sticks.

Here are some low-impact, low-threat ways of bringing the fun (or
funk) back.

Try new and novel things. Get off the couch and do something
different. Find the intrigue. This can show up in all kinds of
different ways. For example, in my family, making kale chips was
novel. Eating them even more so. Read a book from a genre you
don't usually read. Invite someone you don't know well to coffee.
Take a new route home from work. And pay attention to what you
notice and how you feel during the experience or exploration.

Allow for any outcome. People are often surprised by what ultimately attracts and inspires them. Don't limit yourself by precon-
ceived ideas, limiting beliefs, or the opinions of others. Try things
for yourself and then decide whether they are interesting enough
to pursue further.

Do the thing you can't do. Right? We all have things we've
always wanted to try, or things we used to love, but gave up. Now
we are afraid to try again. What if we can't do it? What if we fail?
So often we know what we want to do, but we are afraid to give it
a whirl. Yes, you might fail; then you've gained good information
about what works and what doesn't. Data in. Or you might have an
utter blast, a life-changing experience full of extreme awesomeness.
Either way, you've got a great story to tell.

Whenever we approach life from a different direction, things feel a little bit harder for a while. The routines of the life we know, the schedules and roles we are familiar with, have actually worn those neural pathways into our brains. This makes it easier to do what we do. But when we do something new, when we change things up a bit, those pathways aren't etched in our brains yet. We have to build new ones, new grooves to accommodate the new messages and behaviors. As our brains expand through this process, we might feel uncomfortable, scared, unsettled, and even excited.

Think of learning to play piano, or swinging a golf club, or painting for the first time. Think of writing with your non-dominant hand. New skills are always difficult in the beginning.

Over time, we'll make new pathways, and these new habits will feel easier. In the meantime, all this discomfort can actually be a source of curiosity and fun and exhilaration. Fear can wake us up, and satisfaction emerges when we meet our fear and keep going anyhow.

....

IN THE MOMENT PRACTICE: DO THE BIG, SCARY THING

Think about it. What is one thing you've always wanted to do, but have been too afraid to try? Starting a blog, acting on stage, ice skating, taking a volunteer trip, running a marathon, learning an instrument, starting a business?

Identify that one thing. Then write down one action item—a baby step you can do today in less than five minutes—to move you closer to that one thing.

Now do it! Then, tomorrow, take another baby step, and keep going until you've actually completed The Thing. You might end up disliking this thing you've always wanted to do. Or it might be something you'll try again and develop a passion for. Either way, that's good information. Uncovering your passion often means discovering

*what you don't like. Then, when we do find the thing that
lights a little spark, it's easier to identify.*

....

Think of the discomfort as growing pains. Passions spring from
an internal energy. They do not necessarily emerge from what we
already know or can accomplish easily. When difficulties arise, that
doesn't mean you're off track. It's simply part of learning and part
of living with passion. And if you're feeling a little excited, or even
nervous, you might just be on the verge of something interesting.
Those feelings usually rise up when we are intrigued, and they
could be a sign that you are headed in a direction worth exploring.

Stop talking, planning, and deciding and get moving. Passion
is not passive. You've got to get moving—intellectually, emotionally, physically. You must show up and participate. Stop talking
about the things you've always wanted to do and do them. Take
a class, go on a trip, start writing the book, begin painting, or go
back to school. Make a decision and get going.

The best way to find your passion, and therefore your purpose,
is to stop worrying about finding it and start living it.

LIVING A LIFE OF PASSION IS NOT FOR WIMPS

Too often we expect passion just to show up, to magically appear
and direct our lives. We get restless and frustrated when we don't
know what we want to do when we grow up or when we can't
put a finger on the thing that excites or animates us. We become
impatient when things feel hard. We want someone to tell us what
our passion is.

That's not how it works, people. Passion rarely shows up like
a bolt of lightning or a cartoon light bulb flashing overhead. No
one can tell you what you should love. It is something to be chis-
eled away from the other moments of your life until it reveals itself

as interesting and captivating. Of course, you must be present, authentic, committed, patient. It requires discipline, practice, perseverance, and time.

And don't be thinking it's all good and easy when you finally do uncover your passion. When you find the thing that drives you, you won't always want to do it. You probably won't even be all that good at it. In fact, sometimes you'll actually curse the compulsion that won't let you go. (Think golf.)

Here's how it works. You are passionate about animals, and you love your pups at home and the shelter where you volunteer. Until it's raining and you have a stuffy nose and a headache and the dogs need to go for a walk and then they roll in a mud puddle and now they need a bath and all you want is a cup of tea and a pair of sweats and no muddy paws on your legs. Screw passion; you just want a break.

Or you love golf. You love the group you play with, the friendships you have forged, and the way the game challenges both your mind and body. Until it's cold and you slice the ball off the tee and lose it in the rough and finish with a score of 123, even though you just had a lesson last week. And the game is so hard and your improvement so slow. And you never want to play it again. Not after today. Until tomorrow. Maybe. Maybe tomorrow. Just nine holes. Tomorrow. Yes, probably. Tomorrow's round will be better.

THE MYTH: IT'S EASY; PASSION SHOULD COME NATURALLY

One of the best professional experiences I have ever had was writing my first book, *Imperfect Spirituality*. Loved it. Also, hated it. Sometimes in the same day. Much of the time while I was writing, I also dreamed of working at a sub shop. I am so not kidding. I am a very good sandwich maker. I love sandwiches—who doesn't, right?

The thought of putting a sub together seemed so much more

doable and sensible than writing a book. I knew I could make a sandwich. After all, I've done it before. Lots of times.

Write a book? Never done that. And there were many times—scores—when it was so doggone hard. But at exactly the same time—and here's how passion works—I knew completely that I couldn't *not* do it. I was compelled. So, I sat down and put a book together word by word, page by page. And as time went on, I got better at it.

We are more likely to learn and practice and sometimes even master—though there is always room to improve—the things we are passionate about, because we usually spend more time doing them.

We are constantly improving because we are constantly practicing. Ultimately, this creates a certain level of mastery and expertise that makes our actions look easy.

Ever watched LeBron James play basketball or heard Meryl Streep cop an English accent? Have you watched Bobby Flay whip up a meal in thirty minutes? They make these skills look so easy and effortless that it seems like anyone could do them. We become deluded, then, by their mastery. We buy into the notion that our passions should also be the things we are really, really good at, the things that we have a talent for, or some natural ability. The things that come easily. We don't take into account how many years the masters have put into their practice. How many rough drafts the writers write before you ever see the book. If we struggle with the things we are passionate about, we figure maybe we've picked the wrong thing.

But part of the reason we are passionate about things in the first place is because they are hard. They challenge us, according to psychologist Paul Silvia, who studies people and their passions. Passions generally require an "open-ended amount of skill or knowledge," Silvia says. There is always something else to learn, more to master. We aren't always sure if we'll succeed, and that keeps us curious and interested. That motivates us.

....

Live Well: *Today, do something that feels hard. Finish the crossword, clean out the sock drawer, try a new recipe, or tackle the taxes. Often the most satisfying things are those that challenge us a bit. Take on a small task that pushes you and notice how you feel when you're done.*

....

PASSION IS BIGGER THAN INTEREST

Interest doesn't pack that same kind of punch. I'm interested in a lot of things: I like to golf, play the ukulele, and cook. I LOVE Ducks football. I get fired up about traveling. But none of those things drive me. None of those things propel me through the bad times or wake me up at night (well, Ducks football does on occasion). None of those things constantly challenge me and yet suffuse me with satisfaction and joy and meaning.

Writing does that. Speaking to others about personal development does that. I am passionate about learning and sharing this stuff. It moves me. It inspires me, it gets me going. It keeps me going despite the doubts and insecurities and external factors that make it tough some days.

When you discover what you're passionate about—fishing or cooking, singing or parenting, exercising or filmmaking—whatever it is, it becomes tough to imagine your life without it. Sure, you'll have moments of fatigue and frustration. You may even take breaks from your passion. You may replace former passions with new ones. But once you connect to what you care about, you'll never be far from it, because passion seeps into all corners of your life. It becomes a way of looking at the world and being in it. It demands your attention and captivates your interest and keeps you moving forward.

And that's where you find your purpose.

THE MEANING BEHIND

Purpose is that thing we feel as though we are meant to do. It is the gift or talent that we can contribute to the world. A mission of sorts. It's wholly personal and yet universal, because in expressing it, we impact others.

When one person lives with purpose, it touches everyone. Purpose gives our lives meaning, defines who we are, and helps us know what we care about. To some degree, purpose clarifies the role we'll play here on Earth by revealing the abilities, talents, and qualities we have to offer—the things we use to express our purpose. When we live close to our purpose, it feels natural and right—as though we're doing just what we're meant to do.

Purpose often grows out of passion. When you are swept up by something or in the zone, when you feel totally absorbed by the activity, that is an indication that you are closing in on your purpose. But passion can also explode from purpose. When you are on a mission, focused on a single point, you are more likely to be inspired by the things you must do to fulfill it.

LIVING YOUR PURPOSE

I can already sense the panic:

"But what if I don't know what my purpose is?"

"I don't know what the heck I'm supposed to be doing with my life, and I sure hope my purpose isn't in annual reports and waiting tables and unloading the dishwasher. Aren't I meant to do more?"

Of course you are. And you are already doing it—right smack in the middle of waiting tables and writing reports and completing the household chores. Your purpose is there too. Just because you don't know what your purpose is doesn't mean you aren't already living it.

Purpose isn't a job. It isn't a role you fulfill to the end of your days. It's an expression of all that you are, and it shows up in myriad ways throughout the span of your life.

Power Up: Purpose is an expression of your desires, skills, innate talents, and abilities. It is an expression of your passion and authenticity and values. It is the thing you feel you are meant to do—but it is not limited to one single expression. The way you express your purpose may shift with the seasons of your life, but your purpose will remain constant.

Here's how it works. You are passionate about being a mother and believe your purpose is to raise compassionate, contributing children. So what happens when they grow up and move out?

No worries, because your purpose was never limited to raising good kids. As big as that is, it is much too small for your purpose. You've got more to give. Parenting was merely an expression of your bigger mission.

Your authentic purpose may really be to teach and guide and inspire. It may be to help people realize their value and potential. Right now, this purpose shows up through your parenting style. But as life shifts and changes, you'll find that purpose emerges in different ways. In fact, you've probably been living it all along.

Perhaps you think your purpose is creating art and you are passionate about painting. Your purpose can certainly show up in your portrait work or the landscapes you paint. But your purpose may actually be bigger than creating art. Art may be an expression of your purpose, but your soul-level mission might be to help others know beauty.

Power Up: Your purpose is always bigger and more significant than you think.

....

PERENNIAL PRACTICE:
GETTING CLOSE TO PURPOSE

To become clearer about your purpose, you've got to look at what you are doing when you feel the most authentic, inspired, and passionate.

Recall a moment when you felt awesome, on fire with energy and meaning. A time when you felt like you were making a difference. Where were you? Who were you with? What were you doing? What abilities did this require of you? Detail all aspects of the experience, and write down the skills and talents you have that helped.

For example, say you felt great when you were volunteering in your child's classroom. While volunteering, you really felt great when you were able to help the special-needs kids with reading. With your patience, compassion, intelligence, and humor, you were able to connect and communicate with those students in a meaningful and productive way. You were able to teach them, and they experienced the joy of learning.

Once you've identified those skills, talents, and abilities that showed up during that great moment, go deeper yet. Consider the other times you've drawn on those same skills, talents and abilities.

Back to our school volunteer example: Maybe those same skills show up when you are supporting your partner through adversity at work or a health crisis. Maybe you use that patience and compassion while helping your daughter or counseling a friend who is in trouble.

Look for the pattern. What shows up when you remember the times you felt like you were making a meaningful contribution? When you felt aligned with your values and desires? When you felt authentic? When you go through that inventory of experience, what three or five things continue to show up in each moment?

These things are an expression of your purpose. Your purpose, then, is the overarching quality that brings them all together.

Now, if you want a little extra credit, write down some roles, jobs, hobbies, or tasks that you do now. Write down those that you might be interested in doing in the future—things that would also allow you to express these skills, talents, or abilities. Look at the list. Look at all those possibilities. They are always expanding.

....

Here's how it showed up for me when I did this exercise:

Some of the best times for me are when I learn something new and can convey that information in a way that helps empower or excite others. I love deep discussions. These patterns ran through each of my experiences: communication, writing, connection, learning, teaching, big ideas, personal growth, support.

These things show up when I give workshops or speeches and in the materials I write. They are also there when I'm connecting deeply with friends, when my daughter tells me her secrets, or when I volunteer at school. And the overarching quality is that I want to share these ideas with others. My purpose, I believe, is to inspire, uplift, inform, empower, and connect with others.

I used to believe that writing was my purpose. So imagine the freakout I had when I had a communications job that I despised and went through a period where I didn't want to write anymore. Ever.

Then I realized—eventually—that writing is simply one expression of my purpose. Now I do it in a way that aligns with my values and mission. I am passionate about it again. But I know too that I express my purpose in many other ways.

ACCESSING ALL THIS AWESOME

Think big. Your life's purpose is not a small thing. It is vast and cannot be limited by a single definition or role. This is awesome, of course, because you are capable of living all that. In fact, you are the only one who can. What you have is unique. A distinct combination of intelligence and desire and imperfection and energy. You are the only one who can express this purpose just as it must be expressed. Take it on. Think big and maximize your awesomeness.

Let go of control. Stop trying to control the Universe, your spouse, your computer, what people say on social media, how they drive, and everything else. We can crush our expression of purpose if we create too many rules around it. If we try to plan, predict, or micromanage every move or decision, we are stifled. So stop doing this.

Control is constrictive. Limiting. When we get stuck in the frustration that comes with unmet expectations or we begin sabotaging our awesomeness, it keeps us further from the expression of our purpose and makes us feel like eating an entire plate of brownies.

It is our responsibility to do things each day that allow us to embody the full expression of who we are. No matter how external conditions appear, we can still live on purpose.

Get comfortable with that idea, and you'll see plenty of ways to do it. Then you don't have to worry a bit about how things will happen—you need only be open to all that does happen.

Engage with purpose. While your purpose may remain consistent throughout your life, the way you express it is bound to change and shift. Give conscious thought to how you express your purpose and look for new ways to share that aspect of yourself. If you are in a funk, go behind the scenes to understand why. It could be that you're acting inauthentically or that you're separated from your values and talents; these things can keep you from purpose.

WHEN LIFE ISN'T ALL THAT AWESOME

It's awesome when we go all Carol Brady and live with our passion and purpose. And I'd also like to wake up twenty pounds lighter after a good night's sleep. Not going to happen. I get that. We have to face some crap in the world. Sometimes we hate our job, or maybe our relationship isn't all that.

If we are awakening to our purpose later in life, we may already have some things established—jobs, relationships, responsibilities, habits—that don't support the thing that we discover we most need to do.

This can leave us feeling stuck and tired and murky and dark. If we spend the majority of our time—like on the job—doing something that doesn't allow us to express our purpose or do the things we care about, it's easy to feel depressed. It's easy to become the grouchy old man who lives on your block and wears under-shirts in public while yelling at the kids for being too loud, or the gal at work who takes all her sick time and then uses her smoke breaks to complain about how hard she's working.

I would suggest that you *not* do it this way. Seriously, we don't need any more global mischief or crabby people on the freeway. We need your gifts now. Don't put them off until the kids are grown or you get a new job or retire from the old job or pay your house off. We need you to assume your awesomeness—right now, no matter your job or circumstance—so that we can feel your momentum.

So if you are stuck in a rotten job or limited financial situation or draining relationship—okay, you may have to get a little more creative. The good news is, purpose can be expressed anywhere at any time.

....

Be Awesome: Sometimes, expressing our purpose and passion is as simple as applauding the efforts of others who are doing the same. Cheer someone on today. Check out the listings for a community band performance or high school musical or Little League game and go watch. Be present with these people who are participating simply because they love it. They are risking failure, simply to be a part of something. Root for them. Clap and praise and enjoy watching others participate in their passion despite the risks. It's not how well they perform that matters. It's that they showed up to do it in the first place. That right there is awesome.

....

ACCESSING YOUR PURPOSE NO MATTER WHAT

Your challenge is to find ways to let your awesome out. No matter the circumstances. You can always edge up against your purpose, and when you do, even the most horrid circumstances change for the better.

Here's how to start:

Take a broader view. If you believe your purpose is to protect the environment, but you are working for an oil company, step back and expand your view of your life. Your purpose may not emerge at work. Or it could emerge there in an unexpected way when you begin a lunchroom recycling program, push for green corporate practices, or even take a sack lunch in a reusable container.

Purpose isn't limited by a job description. Make a list of the ways you can express your purpose within those areas of your life where you feel most confined. You may be surprised by how broad the possibilities are.

Make purpose a priority. If your purpose is to live a healthy life and to help others do the same, it's not going to feel good if you are sitting at a desk all day. Schedule time for exercise. Start a walking group at lunch. Or get up early and work out. When you make purpose a priority, you will find ways to express it.

Cut the slack. Maybe the purpose you are compelled to express isn't going to work within the routine you have now. Time to do it differently. Get a counselor to help your relationship; quit your draining job to pursue your passion; shrug off the fears that have kept you from connecting to your bigger expression of purpose.

I'm not saying this is easy. I'm certainly not saying it is always necessary. There are plenty of ways to explore your purpose right now. But if you are ready to change or eliminate the things that don't align with your purpose and values so that you can push yourself into a place that feels better and healthier, take steps to do that, now.

Recognize that you'll be petrified at times. Invigorated at others. You might lie awake some nights worrying and pondering—and then creating. But we all face times like this. Pull from your courage, then, time and time again, to keep going. Be patient too—you don't have to figure it all out in a day. Be grateful for all your previous experiences—even the tough ones—because they have brought you to this moment of possibility.

And know this: If you fail, if it all falls apart, you can still live your purpose. It is not dependent on your success, it is not dependent on how much money you make, how good you look, who you love. It is dependent on you becoming aware and engaged.

Purpose isn't just for people like Oprah. It doesn't have to play out on a big stage or in a marriage or in a major corporation. It shows up in quiet little ways like the way you talk to your son and the way you help others and the way you interact with the natural world. It shows up in the way you celebrate your birthday and what you find funny. It is woven into who you are. You don't have to be famous or wealthy or noisy or college-educated to live on purpose and make a positive difference in the world. You need only express your purpose as often as possible.

Purpose is about you showing up and leaving it out there. When you do that, the Universe will show up in support of you through synchronicity and flow and the energy of awesome.

....

Night Cap: *As you begin to wind down today, consider this: What was one moment during the day when you felt in tune—truly aligned—with your purpose? Capture that feeling in your memory. Now, think of one way you can express your purpose tomorrow at work or home.*

....

ONE PATH: TRUE TO PASSION

Patterns and colors, textures and tones; these are the things that fire up Laura Donaca.

But for decades, Donaca put her passions on hold. Within months of finishing high school, she took an entry-level position in a technology firm. Within a year, she'd moved on to Intel, which then, in the late 1970s, was emerging as a high-tech powerhouse. She started there as a file clerk and steadily climbed through the ranks.

Even so, Donaca's fascination with design and architecture never lagged. Often she found ways to play with her passion even while working at Intel. She was called on to help retrofit office interiors, conference rooms, and other company spaces, and she practiced designing and redesigning her own living spaces.

"I dabbled in wallpaper and picking things out and deciding what goes where and I always thought *Wow, this is so cool, I love this.* I found I have an unbelievable eye that helps me pick out subtle color pigments," she says.

But after more than ten years in tech, Donaca, then in her mid-thirties, knew she had to take a shot at design.

"I had a strong will. I knew I would figure out a way to do it. My boss at Intel gave me flexibility to follow my passion by letting me off work early some days so I could go to school. Then I studied my butt off at night and got up early to study and go to work at Intel. I just wanted it so badly. It was so fascinating and fun."

In her classes, Donaca learned about the history of furniture and how to put together color boards, and though the schedule was demanding, she soaked up all the knowledge. After two years, she received an associate degree and became certified in interior design. By 2001, her shop, L'Donaca Interiors, was open for business.

Donaca now juggles that business around her work at Intel. She often meets clients on the weekends or after hours, which is ideal since most of them have regular jobs during the day, too.

And, the two jobs do share one important similarity—the people. In her roles as a senior administrative assistant and as a designer, Donaca gets to talk with people regularly and really connect with her purpose to make the world a brighter place for others.

Now, after thirty years in the tech field, Donaca is contemplating a transition into full-time design work. The change is both scary and exciting to think about, she says, but she knows her passion will help her persist.

"I'm so fired up when clients call. I want to learn about them, find out what their passions are, what makes them happy, and I want to design that into their lives.

"If I'm passionate, I will do cartwheels to make it happen. I love people and I just walk around smiling and force people to smile at me," she says with a laugh. "I want to make the world better. I know I only have so much control, but I'm not going to stop. So many people walk around with their heads down. Come on, open your eyes, look around and smile. It changes everything and makes every day memorable."

CHAPTER 7:

TAPPING IN TO THE ENERGY OF AWESOME

■ ■ ■

The Master observes the world,
but trusts his inner vision.
He allows things to come and go.
His heart is open as the sky.

—TAO TE CHING,
TRANSLATED BY STEPHEN MITCHELL

It was several years ago now that I was standing at my kitchen sink complaining about my work.

I was only working about ten hours a week, just to make a few bucks, so that I could spend the rest of my time with our then-two-year-old. But the work I was cramming in between other things wasn't all that fulfilling. I was busy, sure, but feeling brain-dead and bored.

"If only I had more time, I would write that book I've been thinking about," I said to my husband.

It sounded ludicrous even as I said it, but I knew I was safe by invoking the *if-I-only-had-the-time* excuse. I didn't have time. I was fitting in my regular work during the baby's naps and a few hours of childcare. There wasn't time to shower, let alone write a book.

So even as I complained, I felt safe. This built-in excuse would save me from my biggest professional challenge yet.

Within twenty-four hours, my plan was foiled when I lost the writing assignments that I did have and was left with nothing but time.

One editor was laid off—it was the beginning of the recession and cutbacks were rampant—and the contract was cancelled. Another changed the terms and I wouldn't agree. Contract voided. Another decided to shift gears and work with a different writer.

Until that day—fourteen years into a journalism career—I'd never lost a single assignment. Haven't since, either. But on that day, when I was asking the Universe for more time to write the work that mattered to me, I got just what I asked for.

The next day, I panicked.

Then I got busy and started drafting the book proposal that would become *Imperfect Spirituality*.

Throughout the entire three-year process, from writing to release, I was guided by intuitive hits, synchronistic moments, and feelings of flow. People, things, and opportunities showed up just when I needed them. I was tapped into the energy of awesome.

THE ENERGY OF AWESOME

Everything is energy, physicists say. The solid world that we see is actually a fluid, permeable, pulsating, vibrating mess of molecules and atoms and subatomic particles, which are all jiving bits of energy.

Our emotions are also transmitted among us through invisible waves of entangled energy. Happiness spreads, and so do negativity and sadness, through an effect called emotional contagion. And even our way of looking at the world changes it. When we give our attention to something, that thing is altered by our attention. Our choices about where to put our energy, then, actually influence outcomes.

This is the world where science meets woo-woo, and I love it. It is evidence that when we can align with the energy of awesome, we can create awesome opportunities, feelings, and possibilities.

Power Up: Everything is energy, and it's all vibrating in distinct and dynamic wave patterns. When we align ourselves with better feelings and the higher energy patterns of love, joy, and peace, we draw more of that kind of energy toward us.

RAISING THE EMOTIONAL ENERGY

It's tough to remember, though, that we can create and live from this higher energy even when the kid loses her coat at school or we accidentally leave the milk in the car after grocery shopping or we get summoned to jury duty. Then it just seems like everything is a hassle. Nothing works. When we have one of those days, our energetic vibrations change to match the madness, and we get more drama and frustration. On those days, we can have the feeling that the Universe is actually out to get us and that awesome belongs to others.

In these moments, if you can deliberately raise your energy just a bit, your circumstances will change. You don't have to do it all at once. You don't have to hustle from despair to bliss to change your experience. You can go from despair to frustration, and that subtle shift will change your energy. You can move from anxiety to boredom, and that feels just a little better. And when you feel just a little better, you behave a little better. That alters the energy around you too, and pretty soon, things aren't looking so bad.

In other words, emotions are energy and an indicator of what we are throwing out to the world, so when we are aware of what it is we are feeling, we can choose to shift our emotional energy patterns to raise our own energetic vibration. This helps us not only to feel better, but also to draw stronger, more positive energy patterns toward us.

....

Do Good: *Today, write a note to someone who has made a difference in your life. Tell this person what he or she has contributed and why you appreciate it, and then run frantically to the mailbox (or hit Send) and mail that sucker before you back out. One of the best ways to raise the energy in your life and in the lives of those around you is to give thanks.*

....

This takes conscious effort, and it can be tricky when someone ticks you off or you feel buried in grief or overcome by a blue mood. Remember even during these times—especially during these times—to reach for something better.

I'm not suggesting that you discard, deny, or suppress any emotion. But in that moment of negativity and hurt, take the time to identify what it is you are really feeling. Observe it. When you do, your energy changes. Instead of being buried by the negativity, you see a bit of light, maybe even an upside—or at least less of a hole. From that little bit of light, you can shift from bad feelings to less-bad ones, and you might see a hint of the love and meaning that is there for you too.

Here's how it works. My big lug of a cat died last year. We'd been together for sixteen years, and he understood me better than most of the other males in my life. Not saying he cared; he was, after all, a cat, but he was well aware of where his kibbles came from.

His loss still pings my heart today. But in the midst of this energy of grief, I realized that the depth of my emotion was also a product of the love I felt for him. Observing my own grief allowed me to be present to the pain, but also helped me to tap into the higher energy, the good stuff, that was there too. It didn't wipe out my grief—nor did I really want it to; he was an important being in my life—but it did move the energy through me in a way that created lightness. It shifted me just enough so that the pain became more bearable.

MOVE YOUR BODY, CHANGE YOUR ENERGY

Energy is everything, and that means it is within us too. Nowadays, it's even measurable. Electrocardiogram machines record the electrical impulses in our hearts, nerve conduction studies show the speed of an electrical response in our nerves, and other tests measure electrical activity in our muscles and brains. We are a mass of energy.

It makes sense, then, that if we want to elevate our energetic response, we need to move our bodies, not sit and guzzle down a gallon of coffee. When we change our posture, our energy changes. The way you sit and you stand can have a direct impact on how you feel.

When we assume what Harvard social psychologist Amy Cuddy calls a power posture (see In the Moment Practice: Get Moving below), it changes the chemicals in our bodies, often releasing endorphins and feel-good hormones that influence how we experience stress. This power posture also sends messages to our brains that cause us to feel more secure or confident or powerful.

....

IN THE MOMENT PRACTICE: GET MOVING

Feeling disconnected? Insecure? Anxious? Or are you just bored and having a hard time getting your mojo going? Whatever it is, one of the fastest ways to get unstuck and raise your energy is to move your body. Exercise is the best way to literally get the energy flowing throughout your physical, emotional, and spiritual systems, but simply changing the way you sit or stand can also make a profound impact. Here's how to do it.

1. Stand or sit in a quiet space.

2. Take an energetic inventory. Notice what you are feeling and how it is showing up in your body. What emotions are you experiencing? What are the physical sensations? Identify places where it feels as though energy is blocked—this sometimes shows up as tension or inflammation.

3. Now, take a deep breath, stand up, put your feet shoulder-width apart, square your shoulders and push them back, and put your hands on your hips. Make yourself big. Wonder Woman big and strong. Stand there in that bold position while breathing deeply for two minutes.

Feel any different? This position can invoke power and confidence, and it boosts your ability to withstand stress and face your fears, Cuddy says. That can change anyone's energy signature.

....

....

Be Awesome: *Floss your teeth. Come on. Do it. It's tough to access our awesome when we are feeling sick and funky. And unhealthy teeth often lead to systemic illnesses and infections that make us super sick. So do what your mama said and floss your teeth regularly. Take care of your body and it becomes the vehicle and the tool that helps you bring the energy of awesome into your life.*

....

UNDERSTANDING YOUR INTUITION

Once you are aligned with these higher vibrating energies like optimism and joy and love and enthusiasm—once you are fired up and aware— you are also more open to new ideas and intuitive hits.

Francis Cholle, author of *The Intuitive Compass,* writes, "Intuition can show up as a gut feeling or a sensation that becomes noticeable without us being fully aware of the underlying reasons for its occurrence."

Intuition is a knowing without conscious reasoning, and it bridges the gap "between the conscious and non-conscious parts of our mind, and also between instinct and reason," Cholle says.

Historically, mystics, psychics, and mothers have had the edge on intuitive insight. (Not kidding about that last one. My mother is crazy intuitive—you know, eyes in the back of her head—and my awareness went into hyper-drive after my daughter was born.) But now the words "intuitive decision-making" are bandied about in every business, from sole proprietorships to Fortune 500 corporations.

It is not a mystical thing, says Scott Barry Kaufman, psychologist and author of *Ungifted: Intelligence Redefined.* Intuition is merely the process of gaining and acquiring knowledge through experience—and then having that knowledge show up for you when you need it.

"The more experience you acquire, the greater your intuition and this connection between your inner and outer worlds," he says.

In this way, intuition is an aspect of intelligence, a part of experiential or implicit learning that is as relevant to achievement, knowledge, and intelligence as rational, analytical thought styles are, Kaufman says.

So the hunch we get—this sense of knowing without knowing how we know—is the accumulation of life experience, knowledge, and awareness that we may not even be conscious of until it rises up through our senses.

ACCESSING YOUR INTUITION

Tapping into all aspects of our intelligence, including our more spontaneous and experiential side where intuition resides, is just plain smart.

If you're going to build a birdhouse, you need a hammer and nails, a good amount of wood glue, some oversight from the guy at the hardware store (though my husband denies this), and, at least in our family, some green and pink paint. If you have the nails but not the hammer, it's going to be a bit more difficult to make a birdhouse and it probably will result in some crying. But if you have the tools available, the work goes faster and smoother, you turn out a better birdhouse, and the process is bound to be a lot more fun.

Intuition, then, is a tool. It is one aspect of our whole self, our intelligent being. Use it along with your rational mind, your physical senses, and everything else you've got—including the hardware store guy who can give you some advice—and you can do awesome things.

Power Up: Intuition is a way of connecting our internal and external knowledge so we can work with our rational, more analytical intelligence as well as our implicit knowledge to make decisions that help us pursue our goals. Understanding how that intuitive knowledge is expressed within you and through you is important to getting information you can use without screwing everything up. When accessing your knowledge reservoirs, then, pay attention to insights, sensations, and ideas that float up. Evaluate their accuracy so you can identify what works the next time around.

Our ability to shift and adapt our thinking styles to meet the demands of our daily responsibilities and long-term goals is an aspect of our awesomeness. Drawing from our intuitive insight, then, can help us make better decisions, act more compassionately, and access the opportunities and knowledge we need to keep moving. It's also a good parenting trick, because your kids are left thinking that you really do know what they've been up to.

THREE WAYS TO CULTIVATE YOUR INTUITIVE INTELLIGENCE

1. **Remember to use it.** There's always more to circumstances than what we can see, so go deeper. We get so stuck in our rational minds that we tend to overthink and overanalyze everything. Instead, pull from the deeper knowledge you've accumulated over the years. Pay attention to physical sensations and emotions. Draw from all of your intelligence.

2. **Notice how your inner wisdom shows up.** Is it a feeling in your body, a new idea in your mind, a question or curiosity that keeps popping up? Insights and information show up in a variety of different ways. Notice how they appear.

In one study, led by Barnaby Dunn at the Medical Research Council Cognition and Brain Sciences Unit in Cambridge, researchers found that people who were aware of their own heartbeat tended to make wiser choices in the experiment.

The researchers concluded that what happens in the body influences how we think. The caveat, though, is to be aware of how you interpret those physical signals. While some study participants were aided by the awareness they had of their own heart, others were led astray by the information because they misinterpreted its signal.

If you notice butterflies in your belly or a tingling in your teeth before something exciting or special happens, take note. Then pay attention the next time you are feeling tingly teeth or butterflies. Perhaps that's a sign that more excitement is on the way. The same is true with other situations. If you notice a tense jaw, or even butterflies, followed by an error, bad decision, or unwanted outcome, next time you feel those sensations you'll have a better idea about how to interpret them.

3.   **Participate in life.** Our intuitive sense is activated when we do new things, expose ourselves to sensory detail, and think about things in a new way. As Kaufman says, the more spontaneous, implicit, experiential aspects of our intelligence are a product of knowledge we have accumulated from life. Start accumulating.

....
IN THE MOMENT PRACTICE: PRACTICE AND PLAY

To get a read on how this energy and insight shows up in your life, you've got to practice with awareness.
Try this:

1.   *Ask yourself a question. Pick something with low stakes. Will my team win tonight? Which way should I drive home? Will the shipment come in time? Or who might be calling?*

2.   *Now, pause for a second to notice the feelings in your body. Pay attention to any memories that show up, and be mindful of your thoughts. Intuitive insight is easier to identify in a quiet mind.*

3.   *Make a note of any outcomes. I like to actually write this stuff down. If I use my inner knowledge to pick a route home, I record anything that pops out at me during the drive, or any thoughts I have. If I guess who*

is calling, I make a note of the sensations I had before
picking up. Right or wrong, understanding how these
insights show up will help you to interpret them now
and in the future, and that is the key to getting infor-
mation you can use.

....

THE SYNCHRONICITY CIRCUIT

Once you are aware of these higher vibrating energies, varied thinking styles, and accumulation of knowledge, awesome, in-spiring, unexpected things begin to happen.

These unbelievable, mystifying, yet comforting outcomes become apparent when we tune in and pay attention. Often they offer guidance, insight, or an "atta-boy" of encouragement that we need to accomplish a task, reach a goal, awesomize our lives. These magical, synchronistic moments usually show up as signs that we are on the right path.

Kevin Kirkaldie wanted to move his family to the Pacific Northwest, but he owned two houses that had to be sold first—one had been on the market for more than six months. Yet, just days after making the difficult decision to move anyhow, both houses sold.

Sherry Beck Paprocki got a book deal, different from the one she had proposed, a few weeks after unexpectedly running into an editor at a writing conference. The editor had an idea in mind that just happened to coincide with Paprocki's interest and quali-fications. The book, on shelves a year later, also helped Paprocki expand her own business in an exciting new direction.

Julianne Barclay connected, a couple of years ago, with a previ-ously unknown cousin through a DNA testing service. After e-mail introductions, the two discovered dozens of similarities and synchronicities, even though the cousin had been adopted by another family and had not previously known her birth family.

Both have five children, including kids from China and Korea. Both have adopted children with special needs. Both women are writers who are passionate advocates for children.

DEFINING THE UNEXPLAINABLE

Synchronicity, a phenomenon that was first studied by Swiss psychologist Carl Jung, is defined as meaningful coincidence. It is a collision between our outer circumstances and our inner thoughts, and for most of us, the resulting experience is intriguing, encouraging, and validating.

You know what I'm talking about: those moments where your feelings and thoughts merge, without any apparent cause, with some external condition or happening or event.

You think of a friend from the past, and they call.

You decide to look for a new job, and someone inexplicably asks if you know of anyone looking for a position just like the one you had in mind.

You think about earning extra income, and you find a dollar on the street.

When these moments happen, they are powerful and mystical and awesome. Synchronicities remind me in a big way that there is a higher energy at work, one that will support me when I'm on the path of passion and purpose. Of course, they also show us when we're not on that path.

Synchronicities validate our experience, but they are not necessarily a culmination of our desires. For example, when I worked in public relations, I had a lucrative account. But I also had the nagging, intuitive sensation that the client and I weren't a good fit. From the very first day when we signed the contract, things went haywire. I made mistakes; his communication system went down and he didn't get my messages; he missed meetings; third parties lost printed material; my car even got ticketed when a meeting I had with the client went five minutes long. It was a debacle. Every time I turned around, my early inner feelings of *whoa, don't do this, this is a bad deal* were supported by synchronistic moments proving the point.

EXPANDING WITH EMOTION AND MEANING

Yet the true power of synchronicity is not in what happens, but in the meaning you ascribe to it.

So, when I was whining about not having time to write a book and then within twenty-four hours I had the time I needed, that was heavy. Seriously. It was like the Universe smacking me upside the head and saying "Hey, dude, now you've got the time. Get busy." And I did.

When Kirkaldie sold one of the homes that had been on the market for months, it was confirmation for him that he and his wife were making the right decision by heading west.

Both events, my losing the writing assignments and Kirkaldie's sales, were pivotal, meaningful moments in our lives. But we could have just as easily overlooked those opportunities and not even noticed the synchronous support.

What is meaningful to me may not matter one bit to you. Synchronicity is highly personal and open to your interpretation. Yet most of us do marvel at stories of meaningful coincidence. They are powerful, inexplicable, and carry a resonant emotional charge.

KEEPING YOUR EYES PEELED

You'd better pay attention, then. Synchronicities can be bold or subtle, but they are always dependent on your noticing. This is the awareness thing coming up again. When you are tuned into the subtle experiences and insights and events and threads of your life, you are in touch with the energy that is guiding you, and synchronicity is part of that energy. This is the thing that gets me fired up and excited. When we experience synchronicity, it is a reminder that we are part of the same energy that made the stars and the oceans and pizza and all the best things in life. We are part of that energy. We are never separate from it—and that is where our awesome comes from. We don't have to know how it works; we can simply trust that it does.

ATTRACTING SYNCHRONICITY

Here's how to do it.

Become aware. Notice the happenings in your life. Pay attention; be present and mindful. Pick up on the textures and subtleties of each life experience. Until we slow down and appreciate each moment, we'll miss the synchronicities, and just about everything else. When you are open to and accepting of whatever appears, you are more likely to experience synchronistic moments that can infuse your experience with meaning.

Believe in the possibility. There is much we don't and can't yet know about higher consciousness and the Universe we live in. When we accept that and open up to the notion that anything is possible, our lives expand. To do this, practice a flexible mindset, one that allows you to move between analytical thought patterns and more abstract ways of thinking.

Embrace the feeling. Synchronicities are often associated with times of high emotion, so pay attention to what it is you are feeling. Often we want to numb ourselves to the so-called negative emotions, but if we can experience them—just sit with them and get curious about where they are coming from—then we create movement and expansion, and that is a breeding ground for synchronicity.

Feel inspired. Inspired people tend to be more creative, driven, motivated, and open to new experiences, according to Kaufman and others who have studied inspiration. They have greater well-being. When you are expanding into your life, not only are you likely to feel inspired, but you will also be more likely to experience synchronicity and other opportunities that will keep the inspiration flowing.

IGNITING INSPIRATION

Kaufman writes that "inspiration is best thought of as a surprising interaction between your current knowledge and the information you receive from the world."

But it doesn't just show up—don't I know it—because you say you are ready. You cannot will yourself to be inspired. And I should mention here that drinking twelve cups of coffee and slamming your head against the desk doesn't seem to bring it on either.

"To be inspired," says Susyn Reeve, co-author with Joan Breiner of *The Inspired Life,* "is to be awake to our unique gifts, talents, skills, and abilities—and to understand that we are part of a larger evolutionary process that calls to us from deep within to be mighty expressions of love in the world. To be in-spirited is to acknowledge and accept our full co-creative partnership with the Greater Field of Life—listening deeply to and being guided by the still small voice within."

An inspired life, then, is not only a product of what we do, but also of how we feel, love, create, think, experience, and engage with our spiritual self and with the world.

You may not be able to choose when inspiration hits, but you can certainly create the conditions that increase your chances of being inspired, Kaufman says.

POWER UP: Inspiration is not manufactured—it simply happens. But you can increase the chances of it happening to you; you can improve the possibility that you will feel inspired by laying a foundation of engagement, participation, and awareness.

THREE WAYS TO FIRE UP YOUR INSPIRATION

1. **Make a good effort.** Get to work. Take action. Learn what you need to know to master the job.

2. **Keep an open mind.** The more open you are to new ideas and new experiences, the more likely it is that you'll be inspired.

3. **Connect with inspiring people—role models, masters, artists, and others.** No-brainer. We feel excited, uplifted, and inspired when we are around good people who are doing good work.

Taking even the smallest step toward your goals and celebrating the little accomplishments along the way can also be a powerful motivating force.

INITIATING INSPIRED ACTION

I will say this: It's unlikely that you will be struck by inspiration when you are lying like a slug on the couch with your face nose-deep in Häagen-Dazs. Unless, of course, your job is to develop ice cream flavors—then you're just all kinds of awesome anyway.

You're less likely to be inspired by sitting in a dark room by yourself. The kind of synchronicities, intuitive hits, and inspirations that add to the energy of awesome, boost creativity, enhance well-being, and make you feel as though you can leap small buildings in a single bound—or at least get a load of laundry folded before dinnertime—require, well, energy. You've got to put in some effort. You want good energy? You've got to put some energy out to get it.

Get up. Move. Create. Risk. Play. Awesome doesn't happen without action.

Still, you don't have to sell the house, change schools, quit your job, or create a masterpiece in a day to live the energy of awesome. You simply need to take baby steps in the direction that you want to go. Inspired actions can be tiny or massive, but they keep you moving.

Here's how it works. You want to return to work when your youngest heads to kindergarten, but you aren't sure what it is that you want to do. It certainly isn't the ten-hour-a-day corporate grind you left when you had kids. No, you want to contribute, give back, make loads of money, and look good while doing it.

One day, you think you might like to be a marketing consultant helping sustainable businesses, but right now, when a good day means changing out of your sweats into actual pants, the goal seems a little far out. It seems overwhelming and impossible, when you look at it from the endpoint.

Stop doing that. Instead, start at the beginning. Take baby steps. After you have the ultimate goal in mind—a fulfilling consultant's position with a flex schedule—put your focus on the one little thing you will need to do today—right now—to get there.

Today, that might mean rifling through the files to find your old résumé—first mission accomplished. Then, maybe next you'll revise said résumé. Another time, you'll evaluate what classes or training you'll need to update your skills. Then, another day, you can sign up for them.

Baby steps, people. One step at a time in the direction you want to move in. You'll feel like you've accomplished something after every benchmark and you'll be inspired to do more.

A PLAN FOR INSPIRED ACTION

Not sure how to start? Try this.

Draw inspiration from others. Get your mind primed for inspiration by taking a few minutes each day to read an uplifting story about an individual who is making a difference, or to find an inspiring role model, or to put yourself in an environment that invokes awe, and you're bound to feel more inspired. It's there for you if you seek it out.

Use your imagination. Pull out a piece of paper and, as quickly as possible, write down anything that you can think of—no matter how small—that will move you closer to the job, or the business, or the relationship, or whatever it is you want. Just scribble it all out—you can even doodle cute pictures. Do this for five minutes. Don't judge what you write, just go. At the end of the five minutes, pick one to do today.

Drop the how, remember the why. After making your to-do list of baby steps, make the first move, without worrying about the second. Often taking one action will illuminate the second. Our path may veer or change as we go along, but often that's because we are meeting people or gaining knowledge that makes our path clearer and easier to traverse. Be open to the meandering, but keep taking those steps. As long as there is movement, you will know what you need to do next.

Keep going. Persist. Make an effort. Put it out there. I certainly don't feel like writing every day. It's tough going and lonely at times, but just the same, I sit down, whine about it for five, Facebook for fifteen, and then I get writing. Always. After about ten minutes of writing time I'm usually so deep into the process that I'm not struggling anymore.

On the days when you are having a hard time making those cold calls, or sending out letters, or making dinner, or packing the lunches, just keep going. When we are active and involved, even if it feels mundane, we create space for new, more inspiring things to show up.

MOVING INTO FLOW

Ahh, here it is, then. The ultimate energy of awesome: Flow. This is what we want to feel. Flow is the feeling that comes when you are fully engaged and absorbed in an activity—especially a creative endeavor or a challenging but intriguing task. When we experience flow, it feels as though everything is going just as it should. It's all coming together. There is a harmony among parts; synchronicities illuminate our path. Life feels natural, free-flowing, effortless, awesome. Time slips by and we are so captivated, so immersed, that we hardly notice.

Famous flow researcher and psychologist Mihaly Csikszentmihalyi described it as the "optimal experience."

Meditation can create this. Basketball can invoke flow. So can writing, painting, running, cooking, loving, jump-roping. Any experience that has a clear, achievable goal, with room to adapt along the way so that you can achieve it, can move you into a flow state.

We all have some idea what this feels like, yet it's almost impossible to accurately describe. It is the confluence of creativity, inspiration, passion, and motivation in a highly energized state, and it feels like all good things are coming your way. You are in harmony with the Universe.

COMMITTING TO THE ENERGY OF FLOW

Like the other energies of awesome, flow doesn't come into play without your participation. Without your willingness to act, you will have no flow. You must be brave, try new things, and be willing to face up to challenges, to live with integrity, and to persist and learn and laugh and grow and trust.

In *The Power of Flow,* authors Charlene Belitz and Meg Lundstrom say that in order to live a life that includes flow, you've got to step up and commit. Make a commitment to personal growth, to your values and the things you care about. Make a commitment to compassion and connection and the other qualities that help us touch others. When we live with the energy of awesome, it becomes clear that we are all one—all connected balls of energy bouncing off each other. What you do, then, impacts me in a very real way.

When you commit to living an awesome life, you tap into your higher energies, and not only will your life open up to greater possibility, peace, and harmony, but you will infuse the rest of us with that spirit. Imagine if we connected to each other only through love and compassion and the energy of joy. World-changing.

This is the power of passion and purpose. This is the reason to persist. This is why we must align with the energy of awesome and notice the intuitive intelligence and synchronicities and flow states that are there to help. This, right here, is the fun part. These are also the qualities that will sustain us when things aren't going all that well, when we've failed, been rejected, hurt. The inspiration that lifts us up to create awesome in our lives will be there too when we feel like we are falling apart and falling short.

....

PERENNIAL PRACTICE:
REMEMBER THE CONNECTION

It's easy in the confusing, frenetic pace of life to think that we are the only ones who aren't intuitive. We are the ones who aren't lucky enough to have synchronistic experiences. The one person on the planet who is unable to experience flow.

Of course this is baloney. But, if you are feeling this way (and we all have), it's probably because you haven't been paying attention. As you pause in your day now, take a minute to ask and answer these three questions in your journal. Relax. See what comes up. I'm betting you'll be surprised.

1. *Remember a time—a brief moment or an extended period—when you felt like everything was working. Everything was awesome. What were you doing? What did it feel like? How did time pass? Did anything unexpected show up in your life that guided you through the experience or added meaning?*

2. *Consider a time when you had a feeling about something and you followed that feeling—or not. What happened?*

3. *Now, think of a time when you read something, saw someone, or experienced something that lifted you up and motivated you to keep going even when it was tough. What was it that inspired you? What made you keep going? How did you feel when you persisted through the difficulty?*

Often, we simply need to be reminded that we are part of all this awesome energy. That it is there for us too. It's like buying a new car—we pick a model and we see it every-where. When you go looking for this energetic guidance, it will show up for you too, just as it has before.

....

....

Night Cap: *Take a deep breath, and in your mind's eye, think of an amazing performance you've witnessed or a powerful story that made you want to do better. Perhaps it was a time when you saw someone do their very best, or one when you watched someone prevail despite great adversity. Settle in with the memory of this event. Reflect on the details.*

Calling to mind an inspiring event or person is one way to draw inspiration into our own lives.

....

CHAPTER 8

FAILING WITH PANACHE

It's failure that gives you the proper perspective on success.
—ELLEN DEGENERES

When I waved at my daughter's bobbing head on the bus yesterday, she caught my eye, then looked away. She was alone in the seat, forehead against the cool of the window.

Something was totally up.

I found out later that she was embarrassed. Sweet P didn't want me to see her sitting alone. Didn't want me to know that a moment before her friend had refused to scoot over and make room for Sweet P to sit.

I listened to Sweet P tell her story. She sat on my lap and cried. I was cool about it. And while she talked and I held her and listened, I also imagined hauling that punk kid off the bus by his size-six jeans while screaming "Nose-picker!" Yes. I know. Don't judge.

I opted not to go with the plan that would have landed me in the slammer. Instead, when the tears stopped, Sweet P and I ate cookies. She told me how icky it felt to be rejected, to be pushed aside. How hard it was to feel left out. She told me that it hurt her heart.

And I hugged her. Then I projected all my junior high angst-ridden experiences onto her. Then I worked through *that*. I told her about the times I'd felt rejected and left out. The times I'd failed, gotten my feelings hurt.

In the end, a few laughs followed the tears. And we moved on to homework and chores and playtime. I'm sure we'll do it all again in a couple of weeks, because rejection, failure, setbacks, social isolation are all part of life. Not fun, for sure, but a distinct part of being human. It's when we develop the skills to manage those moments and use them for positive growth that they also add to the awesome in our lives.

WHY REJECTION HURTS

I know I'm the positive pick-me-up girl and that this is the part where I should say every setback has meaning. Failure helps us grow. Adversity provides contrast so we can appreciate the good stuff in life. I get it. But that stuff doesn't make us feel better in the moment when there isn't a seat for us on the bus. Or a promotion. Or when the one we love doesn't love us anymore. Or when the editor says "No way," with the implied "you suck" close behind.

In fact, social exclusion and rejection, including the self-made mistakes and failings that chip away at our confidence, can actually hurt as bad as physical pain. You can feel as though your heart is breaking when your feelings are hurt. Rejection, exclusion, disappointment, and failure make us ache.

University of California, Los Angeles social psychologist Naomi Eisenberger says the social pain caused by exclusion or rejection is actually processed by the dorsal anterior cingulate cortex and a bit of the anterior insula, the two parts of our brains that also process physical pain.

When we get our feelings hurt or our hearts broken due to social rejection, our brains also release natural painkillers into the body, just as they would to ease the pain of a physical injury, according to research by the University of Michigan Molecular and Behavioral Neuroscience Institute.

This physical reaction to emotional pain may be part of our evolutionary wiring. In the cave days, members of the clan were dependent on one another for survival. If you were cast out of the group, chances are you wouldn't last very long in the wild terrain, so the pain of rejection may have motivated people to form stronger protective social bonds and to avoid situations that would cause social expulsion or rejection, Eisenberger says.

But if you've ever had a job, loved anyone—especially a cat, pursued a goal, or taken a breath of air at any point in your life, if you have ever survived a blind date or slumped against the lockers in middle school, you know that rejection, exclusion, failures, and failings are part of life.

That's the good news, sort of. We are not alone, abnormal, or otherwise messed up if we've failed or been rejected. We are human. Since no one is exempt from this kind of heartache, I advocate two things—other than chocolate.

1. **Stop being afraid—or be afraid if you want, but don't let it stop you from creating the kind of life you'd like.** Sure, you may need to whine and fuss and complain with the girls. You might need to switch course, get up, and try again. Do all of that, absolutely, then keep going. Life is in the participation, not in the outcome.

   To me, playing it safe all the time is scarier than having some emotional bumps and bruises. Staying small, keeping quiet, and not engaging in the things that make your soul sing because you may lose, be dumped on, or get called a fraud is a much greater loss than being rejected and moving on.

   Do not, in other words, crawl up into the shell of a life like a hermit crab when you feel afraid. That is a cramped, smelly, cold way to live.

2. **Know you can survive it.** You can. Seriously, no matter how grandiose the failure, no matter how bad this gets, you will get through it. Chances are there will even be a silver lining—eventually. Not saying you're going to like the process. You may hate it, not see a single benefit to your pain. You may be unhappy, miserable, ungrateful. You may put on twenty pounds as you eat your way through it, but you will be okay and one day you will feel a little less bad. When you know that challenge is going to come *and* that you can survive it, you no longer have to worry about it. This is liberating.

Power Up: While we will be changed by failure, pain, and adversity, we can get through it by believing that we can. That belief alone can help you cultivate the resilience needed to do it.

Here's how it works. When I sent my first book proposal around, I expected it to sell. Eventually. Because I am so dogged, I knew I wasn't going to give up until somebody signed on. I also knew that the proposal and I would be rejected a bunch of times. Dozens of times, as it turned out. I didn't like that part. I was disappointed, frustrated. I doubted myself and fussed. But I also kept working. I wasn't stuck in the failures—even as they mounted for more than a year—and because of that I was able to keep working. I learned more, adapted the proposal, and made the adjustments that ultimately led to publication.

My commitment to keep going no matter what also helped me through a soul-rattling time last year when my arthritis pummeled me with pain and limitation. I didn't love it. I did feel despair and frustration. Depression even.

But even during all that, I knew that I would either learn to live better with the circumstances, or I would change them. I knew I would get through this time, because I knew that the time would change.

I hope I don't have to do it again, that's for sure. The experience was all about setbacks and failure and breaking down. It was emotionally draining and physically excruciating. It was also really scary. But by noticing the fear and realizing that life is fluid and ever-changing, I was able to keep going. I kept actively looking for treatments and attitudes and practices that would help. I also reached out to others for more support. All of that helped me to believe I would get through it. I am resilient.

YOU ARE RESILIENT

You are resilient too. No question about it.

Resilience is the capacity we have to withstand, adapt, and cope with stressful, what-the-heck-am-I-going-to-do-now moments of bone-crushing adversity and setback. You know, the biggies—like when your mother-in-law moves in during an illness, or you lose your job just after you closed on the home, or the doctor finds a lump, or your kid gets really sick.

Yet many days we draw from our resilience just to make it through to bedtime. The days when you get a flat tire and the kids are fighting and the only thing you have to eat in the pantry is flaxseed also demand flexibility and strength.

Just as there can be breathtaking beauty, intense love, and awesome moments even when things feel impossibly difficult and hard and sad, there will be times each day when we need to flex and stretch and adapt to the changes and challenges that are always there.

When we do choose resilient attitudes and behaviors and rise up to look the challenge in the eye, we become more skilled. We become better at coping with some of this stuff. It isn't that the pain or challenge is good in itself—divorce, bankruptcy, loss; no, not so good. But with adversity, we are pushed to learn and grow and adapt simply to survive. We become better at it. When you do tap in to your resilience, little by little, to move into and through the adversity, you might as well be putting on your superhero cape, because there is nothing stronger than you in that moment.

....

IN THE MOMENT PRACTICE: BUILDING THE BOUNCE-BACK MUSCLE

Resilient people believe they are capable of coping. This is a characteristic we can all cultivate by noticing the strengths and resources we already have. Take five minutes to sit down and run a personal power inventory.

1. *Write down the strengths you have. Not just the things you are really good at, but also the things that you are capable of cultivating and developing. For example, you may be persistent, or have the ability to ask others for help. You might be a good reader, which means you'll have the ability to learn what you need to know to cope. Write down all of your strengths, no matter how insignificant you think they are.*

2. *Write down the support you already have. List friends and family members, as well as information, supplies, and materials that can help you in a pinch. Resilient people develop a solid support network.*

3. *Write what you can do to meet the challenges you face. What actions can you take?*

Look at your lists and take note. These are characteristics of resilience.

....

CHOOSING RESILIENCE

Some of those resilient qualities are built in. Others are learned and practiced. All can be developed and strengthened. Optimism, for example, is now considered to be more of an attitude than an innate trait. This is good news, even for you pessimists who are, even as you read this, rattling off reasons why you cannot be optimistic.

Optimism, according to positive psychologists, is part mindset and part behavior that people can choose. It is not cheeriness or a good-humored denial or suppression of the troubles in life. In fact, grounded optimists are usually very aware of what's going wrong.

Optimism is simply an adaptive quality that allows you to believe that things can get better, so you work hard to make it so. Optimism keeps you moving, and that fires up your perseverance, which is an aspect of one of the most important qualities of all—grit.

GOT GRIT?

Right about now some of you are thinking that the only grit you've got is in the grout on the bathroom tile. But grit, from a psychological standpoint, is one of the greatest predictors of success. It is bigger than talent, more significant than education, and more important than ability.

Grit is stamina. It's the stick-to-it-ness that helps us persevere toward our long-term—as in years long—goals. It is the "sustained interest and effort toward," says University of Pennsylvania psychologist and researcher Angela Duckworth.

Grit is a kind of composite of qualities that includes passion, tenacity, discipline, optimism, and a growth mindset.

AN ATTITUDE OF GROWTH

A growth mindset, says renowned Stanford psychologist and researcher Carol Dweck, is the belief that our ability to learn and improve is malleable, not fixed. Those who cultivate this way of thinking and believe that they can improve also tend to respond better to challenges. They are more likely to keep going rather than giving up. Dweck's research shows that our intelligence, achievements, and abilities are directly influenced by our dedication and hard work. With a growth mindset, you believe that effort trumps talent.

Here's the most powerful thing, though, about living with grit and a growth mindset: It means you don't have to have everything figured out. You don't need all the answers to be successful; you simply need to believe you can learn them. Then, you get up and get after them.

Power Up: Grit, our ability to persevere over the long haul, is a greater predictor of success than talent or intelligence. Adopt a growth mindset, believe that you can adapt and learn what you need to know to be successful, and you will be developing the grit you need to succeed.

HOW TO GET GRIT

Although a growth mindset is a quality of grit, researchers are only now beginning to understand how we can all build gritty behavior. Here are a few things that can help:

Pursue your passion. It's easier to persevere, despite setbacks, when you are passionate about something. We tend to be so driven and curious about the things we are passionate about that we will keep going despite the adversity. The process, therefore, becomes rewarding in its own right. If you are pursuing an endpoint, say a million bucks, or losing fifty pounds, make sure you are picking activities and experiences that excite you en route to that goal. Passion helps you persevere.

Build in practice time. Get to work. Creating awesome in anything—despite excruciating rejection, embarrassing failures, and challenges to self and psyche—takes sustained effort. Study, train, learn, practice, experience, memorize, revise, adapt, then do it all again, and you'll get better. You will improve. You will also be gritty.

You won't always want to do the work. Neither do I. But choose to be a creator, not a complainer, and do it anyhow. In the end, you'll learn that you have all that you need to create an awesome life.

Inspire the fire. On the days when you are struggling to push through, seek out inspiration by remembering the times when you've done the hard thing and succeeded. You can certainly do it again. Watch an inspiring video about someone who prevailed, or imagine an inspiring role model, and use those stories of success despite setback to rocket you forward.

Laugh. Don't forget to laugh a little—or a lot. Humor is soothing. It takes you out of the drama, sets you solidly in your humanity, and allows you to take on another quality of resilience, *da, da, da, daaaa*—perspective.

....

Be Awesome: *Today, bring some laughter into your life by helping others to see the lighter side. Look up some knock-knock jokes on the Internet and find your nearest eight-year-old or neighbor or bank teller or friend, and crack them up. It's a silly and light and feel-good way to raise the energy of awe.*

....

TAKING A NEW VIEW

Perspective is big. When we can take a more abstract view and look at a situation from different angles, things change a bit—usually for the better.

Here's how it works. You lose your job. Bummer. You go home and begin to slip down the drain of panic by contemplating what it will mean to be without a job and income. That's one view.

You can also take another look and realize that for the first time since you were twelve years old, you have time to figure out what you want to do when you grow up. You begin jotting down ideas and passions and potential new jobs and you get excited.

Or you can move another ninety degrees and recognize that the time away from work will give you more time with your family. Or shift again and move into gratitude for the money you've saved and the unemployment you'll get for a few months while you plan your next move.

None of these perspectives change the fact that you are unemployed, but they all change the way you feel about it. And, when you are able to raise that energy and take a more positive view of the world, even for a moment, you become more creative. This makes you a better problem solver, and voila, you are able to see the financial possibilities and job opportunities where a minute ago there were none.

For some, this shift in perspective happens immediately. For others it can take days or weeks, months even. Shifting perspective, or reframing, is a practice, a habit, to get into. It is an action, something you do, not something you wait for. Challenge yourself to explore life from every angle, and when the troubles come down, you'll be prepared to find the possibilities within them.

Simply knowing that you can do this, that you are adaptive and resilient, will make it easier to reframe the circumstances that are dragging you down.

All this resilience stuff does take some emotional fortitude and awareness. You can't just go and yank a first-grader off the bus because he was mean to your kid. You've got to have a little self-control.

But feeling the big emotions isn't weakness; it is strength. Resilience means getting clear about what you are feeling—anger or hurt, grief or depression, fear or vulnerability—and dealing with that in a flexible, adaptive way. With this approach, you'll overcome adversity rather than creating more.

Sometimes you'll meet that adversity by eating a pound of macaroni and cheese made with the contraband white pasta instead of going to the gym—or maybe that's just me.

I've had days where I wanted to stay in bed instead of getting up and walking on the swollen ankle that feels as though it's been smashed and lit on fire.

I've also tried to ignore the bad feelings by fantasizing about running away to the tropics, where I'd live under an assumed name with plenty of cabana boys around to tend to my every need—which by that time will probably mean oiling my walker and picking up some Ensure at the pool bar.

These highs and lows are all part of it. But if there's going to be muck—and there is—I'd rather move through it than stay stuck. If I'm going to be hurt and rejected and feel excluded and insecure, then you can bet I'm going to move out of that space as fast as possible. With resilience, there is movement. So on my best days, I fuss and moan for a bit; then I get up, adjust, and move on. In the long run, that's just easier.

....

Live Well: *Next time you are about to topple over from grief or fear or stress or sadness, get up and go outside. Stand in the rain. Feel the wind against your cheek. Feel the heat of the sun. Look at the bushes, and the grass, and the clouds scuttling across the sky. Nature is a balm. An* *anti-inflammatory. Research shows that when we look at greenscapes—like grass and trees—our nervous system settles down a bit. Sometimes the key to resilience is doing something immediately to diffuse the stress and clear your head. This trip outside will help you feel better. You can work from there.*

....

....

IN THE MOMENT PRACTICE:
CREATE A GOOD-NEWS FOLDER

Pull out a file folder. Label it "Awesome Stuff."

Then fill it with awesome stuff. Put in the card you received from a friend or a loved one. Maybe a work testimonial or a good review. Write down a memory of a time when you aced the test or maximized the moment and slip that in there. Print out an inspirational quote you like, or a thank-you e-mail you received. Whatever.

Start with three things. Choose letters or mementos that remind you of your awesomeness, and times when you had it all together. Add to the file as the months go on. When you are going through a dark time and need to be reminded of your awesomeness, pull out the folder, go through each item, and remember who you already are—awesome.

....

KNOWING WHEN TO QUIT

Sometimes, though, perspective shows you that it's time to quit. Sometimes the most resilient, adaptive bounce-back strategy you can have is to walk away. I loathe saying this. I'm the one who will read a really terrible book to the end, simply because I don't want to be a quitter. I'll eat a whole plate of bad food, because I've been taught to finish what I start. Not saying this is a good deal, just saying that it's my deal. But as I've gotten older, I've learned that sometimes the smartest thing you can do is to give up on one thing so that you can do another.

If you are pursuing a goal that no longer matters to you, or you've soldiered on despite years of rejections and setback, it is time to move on. If you are sticking to a course of action for years with little progress simply because you've already invested so much time or money in the process, that way of thinking may actually be keeping you from something bigger and better. Plus it's going to wear you down.

Research by psychologist Gregory Miller shows that clutching at an unrealistic goal or insurmountable obstacle causes our stress hormones and inflammation levels to soar, two factors that researchers say contribute to heart disease, diabetes, and other chronic illnesses. Those who give up on a goal that appears unachievable have less stress and experience greater well-being. They also move on to do great things.

Continuing the struggle—for example, pursuing fertility when you are beyond child-bearing age, or holding on to an unsatisfying job when there is no chance for growth or promotion, or attempting a triathlon when you have a back injury—stresses you out and keeps you from things that open you up to more awesome.

Only you can know when the time is right to walk away. But if you are working toward a goal that no longer aligns with your values (which happens, right? Life changes and we care about different things) or your physical capabilities, consider quitting. If you are pushing toward an end goal that is based on the expectations and desires of others instead of what you really want, give it up. Your mom may have loved to have a doctor in the family, but if you hate science and want to throw up every time you see blood there's probably something better out there for you.

When you do decide to walk away, replace the old goal with something that excites you, something that does align with your values and desires. You're still going to face challenge and failure, but you'll be more likely to mark progress along the way when the goal is a better fit.

> **Power Up:** If you are clinging to a goal where you've experienced little or no progress, one that no longer aligns with your values or desires, one that adds little meaning to your life, it may be time to quit. Only you will know if it's time to give it up, but letting go of something that is insurmountable due to physical limitations or changing expectations will free up valuable time for you to do the things that do matter in your life. That can enhance well-being and awesomeness.

COMING THROUGH IN THE CLUTCH

Even when we are embraced by the cape of resilience and wearing the big G for Grit on our belly, even when we have chosen the ideal goal and we have it all going on, it's all going to come crashing down one day.

We are going to miss the shot, fumble on the final play, stumble over our words at the interview, trip on the red carpet. We are going to burn the food, spell the name wrong, forget the words, misprint the number. We are going to choke under pressure.

True, our brains are loaded with information and expertise that we can use to transform, create, and adapt to anything. It is filled with details we can use to perform well, exceptionally well, even—except for one little thing: We can't always access those little details when we need them.

You may have experienced this before when meeting your boyfriend's parents, or before the board meeting, or job interview, or speech, or test. Psychologist Sian Beilock calls this "paralysis by analysis," and it happens when our brains become so consumed with doing everything right during the Big Moment that it actually gets bogged down in worry over every little detail. We second-guess and ruminate, and all that rumination makes it impossible for us to access the information we need to perform well. So we screw up big time.

Distracting the brain, then, from the Big Moment can keep us from micro-managing and freaking out about every detail. Then we operate on autopilot, automatically doing what we've trained to do.

Next time you are feeling the pressure, try whistling or singing a simple tune. Or get physical by dancing or doing jumping jacks or going for a short, brisk walk a few minutes before the task. These activities can help suppress the worry that sabotages our success. Preparing long before we face the pressure of performance or challenge can also help us show up when we need to. That won't keep adversity at bay, but it is one strategy we can use to meet it head-on.

CREATING YOUR OWN SETBACK STRATEGY

That's the bottom line—we can face up to all the difficult moments and use them to create more awesome ones. We can get better at dealing with bad hair days and bullies on the bus and PTA moms who are hipper than we are (heck, they probably don't even use that word, *hip*) and other life challenges. We can practice and play with some of these other self-helpy techniques and boost our ability and our confidence so that we know we can handle whatever life throws in the ring. I know these things work—because I do them all.

Adopt a growth mindset. Alrighty. We've already covered the benefits of choosing to believe you can improve and learn rather than being stuck and stymied by your circumstances. Researchers can even watch this happening in the brain. When we are familiar and comfortable with an activity, our neurons sail along the superhighway of neuropathways in our brain. The habits and behaviors are well-worn into our gray matter, and so our behavior feels smooth and easy during the task.

When we are faced with uncertainty or challenge—which by their nature are things we aren't sure how to deal with—we feel uncomfortable, because our brain actually has to work to create new routes for the impulses to travel to get us through the experience.

This sets up a serious condition, according to my daughter, that causes us to feel as though our heads are going to explode. For her, this occurs precisely at the same time as piano practice. What's really happening in her brain, though, and in ours when we take on something new, is that we are adapting, getting stronger, expanding. So this, people, is a good thing.

Drop the excuses and cultivate acceptance. You can blame others for your failures and setbacks. You can pin your rejection on someone else. You can make excuses for not getting the job done—*I'm too busy, I'm too broke, maybe when my kids are older*—and you can stay stuck, smack-dab in the middle of the drama. Or, and this is liberating, you can accept what is. You can take a clear-eyed look at life and at the circumstances showing up, and then you can deal.

When you blame, hide, deny, or excuse the reality by wishing or what-iffing—"I wish I hadn't married that guy," or "What if I lose my job?"—you are resisting. At these times, you are stuck in the pain. There is nowhere to go from there.

When you accept what is, then you get to choose the next best action to help you deal with it in that moment. Instead of wishing, you can say "I am married to this guy and I am unhappy in the relationship." Then you are free to choose strategies to help you move to a place of greater comfort.

Acceptance is not resignation. It is not an endorsement. It is awakening to what is, and that, my friend, will get you moving toward more awesome outcomes.

Do a belonging intervention. One of our greatest needs as human beings is to belong. We just want to fit in. In fact, it's critical to our survival as a species.

Yet, when we are facing big problems, it's easy to feel isolated. When we feel like we can't cope or solve the problems or deal with the challenge, we somehow feel it's because we aren't tough enough or good enough. We feel as though we're the only ones who can't manage, and then we freak out.

When this happens, it's time to write a new story around the difficulty. Social psychologist Gregory Walton says that creating a "belonging intervention" by writing a narrative around life's trouble spots can help us get through them. College students who did this as part of a study tended to be more reflective and had greater perspective when dealing with difficulties. They also realized that others shared their struggle. They felt less alone. That made all the difference.

By reflecting on your experience, by rewriting your story and taking a broader view, you'll recognize that you are not alone, either. We are all in this together, and we can help each other through the tough times.

Hold hands, give hugs, connect. Our need to connect is so strong that it can help us feel better even when we are in pain. Research from Tiffany Field, director of the Touch Research Institute at the University of Miami School of Medicine, and others shows that appropriate physical touch, such as a hug, pat on the back, slap on the shoulder, or high-five, can boost performance and well-being. Naomi Eisenberger's work shows that holding the hand of a loved one or even looking at a picture of a partner can reduce the experience of physical pain.

We are social creatures; we do better when we are bonding over margaritas or feeling supported through a hug or compassionate touch. Foster a personal support group of friends and family members you can count on. Nurture those relationships by also giving back. When times get tough, let them help.

Take an aspirin. Or you could just ease the pain of rejection with a pill. Because social pain and rejection have a physical component, Eisenberger's research also shows that over-the-counter pain relievers ease the ache a bit. In one study, participants who took Tylenol reported that they experienced fewer hurt feelings than those who took a placebo. So, there's that.

As for me? I'll take a hug over a pill anytime.

STRENGTH IN SELF AND OTHERS

When we stand up and move into the challenges that show up, instead of hiding out and resisting what is, we become expansive. We are free, autonomous, able to respond in a thoughtful, productive way to any situation. We no longer have to worry what will come; we no longer have to fly off the handle in freakout mode or stay limited by our fear. We can just stand up tall, ground ourselves in the moment, and move into life. This puts us in that place of flow, because we are not fighting against what is coming on, but moving with it.

When we can do this, we can help others find their own power. We can support them in their own creation of an awesome life. We can be the ones who inspire.

No one can do it alone; plus, it just wouldn't be fun. But when we know what we are capable of, we are less judgmental and more compassionate toward others. This shift is the way to build community, and when we are coming together, we are less likely to fall apart.

....

Night Cap: *Visualize your superhero self. Think of a challenge, fear, or setback you are facing in your life. Now, imagine yourself as the only one who can wipe out the fear and take care of everything. There is no angst, no self-doubt; you are, after all, a superhero with special powers.*

You look hot in that outfit and wear amazingly awesome shoes.

What would your superhero costume look like? What strengths could you use to minimize the challenge? Imagine, daydream, and play with the idea of your superhero self as you fade off to sleep.

....

ONE PATH: SYNCHRONOUS SOLUTIONS

It had been a rough year for Lorri Dane, but then, divorce is never easy, especially after more than two decades of marriage. Dane was in the thick of the turmoil in 2013 when she ventured into her first yoga class.

"I was just stressed out; we'd had a huge fight, and for some reason, all I could think about what that I needed to find a yoga class," Dane says.

She says she was a "mess on the mat" that first day, but Dane was immediately captivated by yoga. Inspired by the peace and well-being that she felt with the practice, Dane is now studying to be an instructor. And, the yoga classes that helped her regain inner calm also led her to a series of synchronicities that helped her find meaning in the difficult days.

As things began to settle in her personal life, Dane started looking for a new place to live. The lease on her apartment was ending, and with thirty days to go, she was feeling discouraged. The properties available were either too small to share with her daughter or too expensive for a single income. Yet she always had a sense that something was going to come up and that everything would work out.

It ended up working out in a Bay Area bar a couple of days after Christmas. There, while visiting with friends, Dane met a woman, a friend of a friend who hadn't even planned to come, but then showed up at the last minute. As the group was leaving, Dane casually mentioned that she was looking for a place to live.

Turns out, the last-minute arrival was moving out of her home in a few weeks and was looking for a renter. The property was ideal in price and location for Dane and her daughter.

As the two women talked, they discovered other commonalities. Their kids knew each other through school; both women had been through difficult relationships and were now starting anew. They became close friends, and when it was time to move, Dane helped her pack.

"I think it was all meant to be," Dane says. "After my divorce, I just opened myself up because I didn't know how else to do it. I know now I don't have to do it alone and I can't do it alone. I don't have to shoulder the burden. Yoga helped open up those channels.

"I believe that if you just let go, your basic needs will be met. That has happened for me. Life put me exactly where I'm supposed to be."

CHAPTER 9:

ACCESSING THE AWESOME OF OTHERS

No one has ever made himself great by showing how small someone else is.

—IRVIN HIMMEL

It was twenty-six degrees outside, and I marched my family out to the sidewalk in front of our house. They were wearing sweatshirts and pajamas. I figured I had a good couple of minutes before hypothermia set in.

"Come on," I said. "You don't need a coat. It won't take long."

"Mommy, it's freezing."

"Look at the moon."

"I've seen the moon before. My toe feels like it's going to fall off."

"You've got other toes." I turned to my husband. "Honey, isn't it amazing?"

"No other mom makes their kids freezing," Sweet P said.

"Yep, it's amazing all right," said the husband. "I'm going in."

I stood there a minute longer, gazing at the harvest moon. It was stunning, but I'd stayed out longer than I should have just to prove a point: I'm not going to miss the awe in my life. Nor will

I allow anyone else in the family to miss it. We are a Forced Awe household. Awesome things are all around us and we are going to notice them all—darn it!

To be in that moment of indescribable vastness, or deep connection; to experience those transcendent moments of beauty and power and love, to feel all that, inspires us to connect with others. It is a byproduct of the emotion. We experience something so grand that we want to share it.

When we can share it, we are no longer separate from this energy. It is within us all.

To live our awesome, then, we must access that—the power within ourselves and others. We must connect with and love and inspire each other. Sometimes we just need to shut up and let things be and trust that the rough and pockmarked road we are bouncing down now is the one we are meant to be on, and we must allow others the freedom to trip along their own path.

For me to live an awesome life, I must help you live yours. You get this? My awesome is related to your awesome. I can't diminish you as a way of uplifting myself. It doesn't work. I am no better if you fail.

But when I show you the road to your own awesome, when I pinpoint the things I love about you and help you to see your talents, when I believe in you, listen to you, and laugh with you, we both let awesome in.

You can achieve your goals. You can laugh and have fun, have awesome experiences, live with awareness and grit. You can expand the boundaries of your potential, but only when you let all that awesome out, when you express it and let it swirl around me and the others on this planet, only when you share yourself do you inspire me and make it safe for me to live my awesome too. Then we both stand in a place of awe.

This is it—the place where we come together and bring our awesome to life. This is where we change the world.

MAKING ROOM FOR VULNERABILITY

There is a certain degree of vulnerability required to do this, of course. There is a high likelihood that you'll fall on your face at least once. In my case, this is a daily occurrence.

I'm good with it now because, well, I'm used to it. And I know from experience that the only way to awesome is to open to all. To go all in. And when we are there, at the end of the diving board with everyone looking at us, when we are all in with our ideas and our emotions exposed, we are vulnerable. We are soft. This is why we need each other. We must take care of each other, make it safe to do this.

Sure, there will be haters. Many, oddly enough, will not see how awesome you really are. They will get caught up in petty details like appearance and boyfriends and the car you drive and the job you work.

Take the women who are nominated for Oscars every year. Most have spent their lives practicing, training, and studying. Then, they go all in. They do their best work on a single, pivotal film that oftentimes changes how we think about the world or ourselves. They are lauded for those efforts, for a few minutes, and then they are judged for hours about how they look, what they wear, who they are with.

We get so judgy and caught up in what we don't like about one another that we forget how brave we are too. It takes guts to show up, and we must come together and support those who do.

The way to access awesome, then, isn't just to cull it from others—although the give and take is a powerful part of living an awesome life—but to make it safe for others to share their awesome with you.

....

> **Be Awesome:** *Today, be vulnerable. Open. True. Be yourself. Share a secret or a fear or a dream with someone you trust. Express your opinion even when it may not be popular. Be authentic. When you are open about who you are, you no longer have to worry about who you are not. You can love yourself for all of your strengths and talents, quirks and flaws, all of it—and this is awesome, of course—but it also allows you to connect and love others in a deeper way.*

....

FIND THE SAFE PLACE, BE THE SAFE PLACE

To do that, you've got to make room for people to be themselves. You've got to be in that uncomfortable space with them so they can come in and let up and let down and let out.

Here's how it works. Your daughter doesn't get into the school that she wants and she shares her disappointment with you. She cries. Expresses her insecurity and embarrassment over the failure.

It hurts to feel her loss. You want to ease her pain, but you know that she must see her own strength, to learn that she is capable of getting through this and anything else. So you sit there with her, making it safe for her to be real and vulnerable. You do not solve or fix or rage. Nor do you try to quell her emotion. You are simply fully present, and as a result, you make it safe for her to be fully open and authentic.

Or maybe you are dealing with a snarky customer service rep on one of those endless phone calls. At some point in the conversation, instead of being angry about the failed service, you become empathetic. The voice on the other end softens a bit and the situation is resolved.

Or say a friend calls upset over an interaction with her boss.

You are the safe place. She gets to vent. You get to connect, and stress transforms to calm and maybe laughter.

Stranger or partner, child or colleague; we all crave connection. We all want to be understood. When you can be the soft place, the place where people can open up about their shame and embarrassment and stress and disappointment, you also get to be there when they awaken to their awesome.

Find a safe place for yourself too. A best friend, a partner, a support group where you can go when you are scared and alone and failing and falling apart, a place where they will let you be messy and out of control and dumb and hurt and even while you are being all of that, they can still see the awesome that lurks within.

Be Awesome: Next time you meet up with someone—friend, family member, or stranger—presume the best. Be free from judgment and be open to anything in the conversation. Often we look for the worst in people, even those we are just meeting, and that closes us off from the possibilities of goodness and opportunity. Be a believer in the goodness of others and you'll be more likely to find it within yourself as well.

ILLUMINATING THE AWESOME

A couple of summers ago, my body let loose this experience of fatigue and pain and limitation that I hadn't felt in a long time. Inside I felt dark. Kind of rotten, like things were drying up. I was cut off from the energy and the optimism that had always helped carry me through the tough times. I'd run off the road. And it had been so long since I'd done that, I didn't know what to do. I felt shaken and scared.

It was tough to get the work done because the pain made it hard for me to focus. Fear kept me locked in a cycle of what-iffing—"What if this never gets better?" I wasn't sleeping through the night, which meant my patience was shredded. I had problems getting out of bed without help. The pain medication didn't help. A change in diet didn't help.

The stress of the situation was compounded by my own self-image. I study all this stuff about how to feel better in life, about self-acceptance, about creating the experience we want, and yet for a little while, I wasn't doing any of it. I had lost my way.

I don't talk too much about my experience with chronic illness, because I think there is a fine line between communicating about the daily challenges and complaining about it. I don't like to dwell in the energy of complaint, so I usually look for ways to honestly share my experience without ruminating about it. And during this phase, I didn't know how to talk about it, so I shared only a bit with a couple of friends. It was a lonely place.

One morning, I lurched out of bed after having slept only a couple of hours, and I received a text from a friend.

"How is your ankle?"

"Bad. I haven't slept. Can't walk. Sucks."

"I'm sorry. For you to say that, I know it must be bad, because you are one of the strongest people I know."

And just like that, I was stronger. Just like that, a bit of my awesome was illuminated, because someone else saw it in me.

Your awesome doesn't go away. It isn't something you lose. But there are dark times when we can't see it in ourselves, when we need to reach out, seek support, and allow others to help us find our way.

Get the help; then be the helper to someone else. Spend time reminding them of the goodness that they hold within, rather than their challenges or screw ups. We are never the difficulties or the failures or the mistakes or the pain. Those are merely situations we encounter.

Thanks to my husband and some great friends who were brave enough to let me be real and broken down, and due to my own persistence, I came through that time wiser and more grateful. I found people who are helping me heal, one physical therapy or acupuncture treatment at a time. And more than ever, I find myself looking for ways to support the awesome in others, because no matter how hard it is to see, I am sure it's in there.

LISTEN, THEN TALK—OR MAYBE NOT

The first step to supporting each other in this reciprocal awesome love fest is to listen up. Just saying right now, this isn't my strong suit. I'm a talker. I'm an idea person, and I love to blurt out thoughts about everything from meditation and world peace to the best hamburger joints and television dramas. I want to give you advice, because I love you and I want to help and I want the world to be all rainbows and unicorns.

But for an exchange of awesome, I need to shut up and pay attention to what others are saying. That's what we all need to do—pipe down and listen to each other.

You are not listening when you are judging her hairstyle. You are not paying attention when you are forming an opinion about what she is saying. You are not even paying attention when you are looking into her eyes and wondering what kind of moisturizer she's using because she is looking good and you *know* that girl is the same age you are.

We have so much noise in our lives—smartphones, iPods, television 24/7—that we have forgotten how to listen. We have to coach ourselves to become quieter and practice putting all the peripheral stuff down and giving our attention to the things that don't need batteries to run.

"Feeling heard is extraordinary," says writer Jessica Morrell. "It makes me feel quiet inside and the other person usually has a stillness to them. I believe people have a deep longing to be heard. It's healing."

Power Up: The greatest gift we can give others is our attention. Put down the phone. Stop what you are doing. Make eye contact and step into their stories with empathy and compassion. Don't judge what they are feeling; allow them their experiences and move into those experiences with them. Empathy is an awesome way to connect.

When we back away from our own stories and our need to interject and interrupt, to better know the person speaking, we open the door to learning and growth and connection. This exchange triggers our curiosity, intelligence, creativity and inspiration. All that happens when we get quiet and listen to one another.

HOW TO VALIDATE THE EXPERIENCE OF ANOTHER

Ready for all that? Are you ready to step into the moment with a friend or family member or partner or even a complete stranger, to hold space for them, to validate their experience? Alright, here's how to do it:

Ask relevant questions. Do not, for example, change the subject or ask her where she wants to go to dinner when her husband just walked out.

Be present. Tune in. Immerse yourself in the moment that is now. Do not be thinking about whether you set the DVR for the game later.

Reflect. Emotions, words, even tone and gestures. Extend yourself, ask questions using the words you hear him say, or seek understanding by reflecting back detail. "So you are scared because the boss said there were going to be layoffs…" Then just shut up and listen some more. This is not the time to put your words to someone else's experience; it's your time to really hear what they are saying with the words, gestures and tone they use.

Gotta say, sometimes this whole reflection thing sends me over the edge. When I haven't showered and I'm standing at the sink and my daughter is hollering that she's been born into the wrong family and wants a nicer mother and the pipe under the sink blows up leaving the guts of our garbage disposal and orange rinds and slimy spaghetti in a puddle under the sink and my husband comes in and I rattle off a list of my complaints and frustrations and he says in the gentlest, kindest, therapist-sounding voice, "So what you are saying is that you are feeling upset and frustrated and you want to run away," I completely lose my stuffing. I want to rip his head off.

This leaves him in a state of utter confusion, because he was only trying to make me feel heard. But when the sink isn't flooding and we are quiet with each other, working through things, and he meets me with words and emotion and understanding that he has absorbed from our conversation, it's a good thing. It builds connection and collaboration and a lingering openness that wasn't there before.

When someone listens well, says photographer Deborah Dombrowski, "you feel the wall around your heart melting and washing away. It feels like a lily opening inside of you."

The best listeners validate. Instead of turning away from the emotion, they step into it and fill the space with compassion.

EVERYTHING STARTS WITH COMPASSION

Compassion is a game changer. It is a skill; it is a practice; it is a habit; it is a quality that through one small act can uplift and inspire an entire population, end arguments over dinner, and silence a toddler's meltdown. It can get the grouchiest checker to put the bananas in the bag a little more gently and make you feel better when everything is going haywire.

Seriously, if you want a superpower, this is it, people.

When we act with compassion, we are not only leading with kindness, but we are also changing sides a bit, moving on over into the metaphorical shoes of the person we are interacting with. We take a look at the world from their perspective. This is powerful, because it helps us to see that maybe the guy who cut you off on the freeway didn't hate you after all. It reminds us that people behaving badly may be covering up for their own hurt and fear, not just trying to make you mad. When you act compassionately, you get to see clearly and definitively that it isn't all about you.

People can be jerky. No question about it. But when you act compassionately anyway, when you are kind anyway—you not only short-circuit the pain you may experience, but you are also showing the world the awesome that you are. And you are also more likely to see the awesome in others.

Here's how it works. You go to a New Year's party and run into a long-time acquaintance who spends most of the conversation bragging about her business accomplishments and looking over your head to see if someone more important has arrived. You can get all upset over this, you can take it personally and rise to the challenge by interrupting her and talking about your own awesomeness, because we know you've got it going on.

Or you can smile and nod your head and listen and ask questions and connect with her in that moment before excusing yourself and heading straight for the champagne table. This is what you do, of course, because you are living an awesome life.

Weeks later, you get an e-mail from the woman, talking about how stressed she was that night because she was waiting to hear back on a work proposal. She was filled with self-doubt, but after speaking with you, she felt better and more confident. And, by the way, she got the job and has you in mind for a lucrative project. Are you interested?

BARRIERS TO COMPASSION

The payoff with compassion isn't always so clear-cut; the rewards are rarely external. But this is one quality that feels good to give no matter what you receive.

Still, we can be withholding. We can get in the way of our own essential nature and throw up barriers to better living.

Judgment. You think you know better? You think they've got it all wrong? You don't like how they treated you or your service? All may be valid points, but none of it matters. We like to punish and discipline. When people act poorly, we want them to be called out for it.

But you can do it differently. You can hold people accountable and still be compassionate. You can project dignity and humanity. You can be kind. You are either compassionate or you are judging. Pick the one that feels best.

Fear. We don't want to be too kind; I mean, what if people take advantage? Remember, you are a creator, accountable for what comes into your life. Nobody can take advantage of you. Sure, you might feel pain or disappointment. But you can get through the fear by raising your own energy and acting compassionately.

Once you give it out, it's no longer your business what somebody does with it, but you will be free to move into a better-feeling experience.

Busyness. We get so locked in our routines that we rarely lift our heads up to notice unless someone wrongs us or behaves badly. Slow down, in each moment. Look for more than trouble. See the checker taking your money and say thank you. Understand the discomfort of the gas station attendant who is freezing his behind off in twenty-degree weather and reach out with a simple "Take care and stay warm." Let people know you are seeing them and their experience.

It doesn't take more time or money to act compassionately. It takes action and effort and awareness. But when you share your kindness, kindness comes to you in return. When that happens, self-acceptance flows.

SELF-ACCEPTANCE IS PEACE OF MIND

Self-acceptance is like regular acceptance; it is seeing what is without judgment. All fine and dandy when we're looking hot and everybody knows it, but not so easy for us humans when we forget our credit cards in the gym bag and we're holding up the whole line at the grocery store, or we say something stupid and insensitive to a friend in crisis and feel like a schmuck. Been there. Been all of there. Of course I have, we all have, because that's part of being human. We are bound to blunder.

In these moments, what if you accepted things just as they sat?

"I said something that hurt my friend, and I feel bad about that."

Instead of the usual derisive self-talk we saddle ourselves with, like "I'm such a loser, that was a stupid thing to say, but she needs to get over it."

Wouldn't that be a bit more freeing? Wouldn't that level of acceptance allow you to see clearly what occurred so that you could learn from it, take positive action, and move through it with compassion for both yourself and others?

It's not letting yourself off the hook. Self-acceptance simply allows you to see the situation for what it is without inflating the drama with sarcasm and condemnation and attitude. Then you can deal. And apologize too, if you need to.

APOLOGIZE AND FORGIVE

The other night, my husband and I had a disagreement. I can talk about it now because I'm pretty sure he won't read this far. He was doing his thing, tuning out, not paying attention to what needed to be done, and I was doing my thing, being hyper-aware, paying attention to all that needed to be done, and being critical that he was tuning out.

"Geez, I *always* have to do *everything* around here," I said with a dramatic sigh just loud enough for him to hear. Them's fightin' words.

Mr. J is a true partner around this place. He is selfless and diligent, so when I suggested that I do everything alone, he was, er, *upset.*

A discussion ensued. Nothing got accomplished, of course. We didn't solve anything. He was a meanie, I was condescending. And instead of drawing together, we were depleted and separate by the end of the rant. Of course, we also had a kid in the room, so this whole thing happened with strategic comments and a few whispered jibes.

The minute Sweet P was in bed, we finally had time to talk. I was still ticked. But I was also sorry. I'd been a jerk, short-tempered, unfair, and I felt icky about it.

I apologized. He did too. And right then, we came back together. I had a chance to explain, like a grown-up, what had triggered my frustration. He shared his feelings, and we moved into a place where we were actually able to improve things.

The apology caused an alchemical reaction that allowed us to transcend the hurt and frustration and grow our relationship.

So do we get it right every time? Not even close. Sometimes he's just annoying and I'm just grouchy and critical. But when I am able to accept my role in the situation and find my way clear of it, a well-placed, sincere apology is a way to move forward.

HOW TO SAY YOU'RE SORRY

An appropriate apology can provide relief and healing for both the person apologizing and the one on the receiving end.

That doesn't mean blurting out a casual yet sassy "I'm sorry, but..." as you storm out of the room. The word "but" should not make the apology cut if you are looking to repair the damage done by previous actions.

After studying the dynamics of shame, humiliation, and apologies for more than seven years, Aaron Lazare, psychiatrist and author of *On Apology*, says that the best apologies follow these four steps:

1. **Acknowledge your error.** Using "I" statements to show responsibility, specifically acknowledge your mistake.

2. **Offer explanation.** Explain how the mistake occurred, but do not make excuses.

   Try this approach: "I was confused and didn't take time to ask questions before I acted."

   Do not try this approach: "I was confused because you are always overreacting, and so I stopped listening."

3. **Show remorse.** Share how you feel about the error. "I feel sad and disappointed that I spoke to you that way and hurt your feelings."

4. **Make amends.** Apologize again and make a specific statement about what you'll do to avoid repeating the mistake.

   Then, learn to forgive, both yourself and the person who hurt you. Learn to let it go and fill up the space once held by hurt with goodness.

FORGIVENESS FREES YOU UP FOR HAPPINESS

The steps to forgiveness aren't complicated, says psychiatrist Walter Jacobson, author of *Forgive to Win!*, but we have to be willing to do it. There's the rub. We are reluctant to forgive because we believe that by forgiving we are somehow excusing the inexcusable. Our egos connect to the notion that people—ourselves included—should be punished for bad behavior.

So we hold on to the hurt. We hold on to the pain of our childhood, or the betrayal of a cheating spouse, or the hurt of a friend who bailed when we needed them most.

We hold on, too, to the trust we violated with our drinking, or the damage we did when we left the marriage. We hold on to all the wrongs we couldn't right. We edge out the awesome with past pain.

This doesn't mean you've got to be besties with those who hurt you. You don't even need to see them. Forgiveness is an internal process, Jacobson says. There is no need for confrontation.

Instead, he suggests you look at the past hurts with insight and understanding. Ask yourself why you want to forgive in the first place and you'll find strong motivation to do so.

"Unforgiveness hurts you," Jacobson says. "Forgive for your own peace of mind. When we don't forgive, we are recreating our own victimhood and then we get caught up in that. Forgiveness is not letting others off the hook, but it allows you to find your own satisfaction and that is strong motivation to do it."

Like anything, forgiveness takes time and practice. We've got to get in the habit of doing it, of letting go, of choosing acceptance and love over anger and pain. When we do that, we are free to create a more peaceful and joyful life.

To begin the process, Jacobson recommends five steps:

1. **Recognize what you are feeling in the moment.**
   Anger, hostility, judgment?

2. **Disengage.** Stop participating in actions or thought patterns that intensify your need to punish or hurt the way you've been hurt. You may even say to yourself, "I don't need to judge here." Replace the judgment with acceptance and awareness.

3. **Release the hurt.** Consciously let it go. Imagine it leaving your heart and mind.

4. **Replace the hurt with something helpful.** A feeling of peace, thoughts of connection with someone who loves and accepts you, a mantra that shores you up, an inspiring story that connects you with your highest self—something positive.

5. **Keep it up.** You may have to repeat these steps often until you develop the habit. New things may trigger old feelings, and you may catch yourself judging and hurting again. But, when you practice forgiveness, you know you can be free of all that too.

   Forgiveness is the process of letting go of past pain and hurt and replacing them with acceptance and peace. Doesn't that just sound better?

....

IN THE MOMENT PRACTICE: ENDING THE LOOP OF JUDGMENT

Recognizing when we are getting stuck in a loop of judgment and condemnation is part of learning to forgive. When you catch yourself judging, you can consciously choose thoughts that will take you out of that negative space and move you into better feelings.

Jacobson suggests a mantra. When you are judging, try repeating this to yourself: "Anger hurts, forgiveness heals."

If you're like me, you might need to say this a billion times. But while you are doing that, you will not be caught up in the hostilities or the pain. You won't be stuck. Acceptance is possible from this position, and so is benevolence and generosity.

....

GIVE SOME GOODNESS

A couple of days after starting this book, when I was edging up against self-doubt and struggling with the work, I went outside to get a breath of air and found a tiny package wrapped in a paper bag tied carefully with a polka-dotted ribbon. Inside, I found an awesome, sunshine-colored ink pen. No note. Not sure where it came from, though I do have my suspicions. But it changed my energy in an instant.

No question, when I think of awesome, I think of pens and paper. I've had a long-term love affair with both of them. And that little gift broached the isolation I was feeling that day and got me going again. Know what? Every time I pick up that pen, I feel good all over again.

That's what generosity does. It keeps giving. It is a way of connecting to the best energy in both giver and receiver.

Giving, whether it's in the form of verbal support and kindness, time, money, or gifts, leads to a greater sense of well-being and a satisfaction in life. It feels awesome to give to someone else.

Neuropsychologists use a fancy term for this: *eudaimonic well-being.* This is the good feeling, sometimes happiness, that bubbles up from within when we have a deep sense of purpose and meaning. Those positive feelings build when we do good things for others.

Researchers Steven Cole and Barbara Fredrickson studied the response of the human genome—which is a complete set of DNA and genes containing all the body's information—to positive experiences and emotions. They discovered that these very building blocks of the body do act differently in people who have a sense of purpose and contribution.

These people have lower levels of inflammation, stronger levels of antiviral and antibody genes, and stronger immune cells. People with hedonic well-being, the type of happiness that comes from moments of self-gratification, had higher levels of inflammation and lower antiviral and antibody response.

In other words: We are healthier and happier when we make a positive difference in the lives of others, not when we win the lottery.

"At the cellular level, our bodies appear to respond better to a different kind of well-being, one based on a sense of connectedness and purpose," said Fredrickson.

Not only does altruism boost immune function and improve our moods, but those who do good also live longer. And do-good behavior inspires an explosion of goodness. Remembering the gift of the pen, and special chocolates dropped off by another friend, inspired me to give to others in my neighborhood. Little acts make a big difference.

....

IN THE MOMENT PRACTICE:
DO IT NOW

Okay. Right now—well, after you are done reading this—do something for another.

Right now. Write a love note to your partner and hide it for her to find. Send a check to the food bank, call Meals on Wheels and sign up for a volunteer shift, bake cookies or a casserole (but avoid tuna—no matter what my mom always said, nobody likes tuna casserole) for the neighbors.

....

PERENNIAL PRACTICE:
BECOME A DAILY DO-GOODER

Each day, put one item—a random act of kindness—on your to-do list. Try to make it different every day. I write lots of letters to people who may not otherwise get mail. I leave love notes for my husband. Sometimes I volunteer my time at the school or donate money to nonprofit organizations. It doesn't have to be complicated or expensive, but make giving a part of your life.

Put it on the schedule. Have fun thinking up things to do. Then follow through on these random acts of kindness. When you have a moment later, reflect on how you felt about what you did. Journal about it.

Night Cap: *Reflect on a time when someone gave you a gift—when they supported you emotionally, gave you a present, offered a compliment. Allow yourself to recall those good feelings. Then, think of a time when you also made a difference in someone's day. When we remember the power of giving, we are motivated to do more of it.*

CHAPTER 10:

CREATING AN ATMOSPHERE OF AWESOME

■ ■ ■

You can discover more about a person in an hour of play than in a year of conversation.

—PLATO

The teacher was looking at the woman two seats to my left waiting for her to play, but she shook her head no, so he moved on to the guy next to me, who played *Ode to Joy* on his abalone-inlaid instrument. He missed the note in the middle, but I thought he was brave. Brave for giving it a shot in front of the class of twenty-one others in Beginning Ukulele.

When it was my turn, I wanted to shake my head no too and have the teacher move on. My palms were sweating despite the air conditioner, and I kept rubbing them on my capris. I felt fifteen-cups-of-coffee shaky and had lost control of my fingers.

It was the first night of class. Of course the overachiever in the front row who volunteered first had played the piece perfectly. Didn't miss a note. Smiled shyly and appropriately when the class applauded. She was also super friendly and supportive. A good person and a star ukulele player. That's just annoying.

But the teacher was looking at me now, not her, and I wanted to go home, practice for about twenty years, and then come back to class. I was thinking all this even as I felt my head nod yes. *My turn. I'm gonna do it.*

The week before, I'd done an hour-long keynote about optimism and compassion and productivity to a group of one hundred people without a blink. But playing a line of music in front of twenty had me tight and anxious.

I tucked my red ukulele (yes, it's party red) under my arm, pulled it tight against my chest, and began to pluck out the notes. One by one. *Oops, that should have been a C. Try again. Keep going.* And with silent apologies to Beethoven, I finished and could breathe again. That's when it hit—all the awesome of a warm night in July spent sitting with a group of strangers learning to play a red ukulele.

Awesome doesn't show up when you take a pass.

It shows up when you say *Yes, I'll go.*

Power Up: An awesome life does not manifest by default. It shows up when we act, prepare, and create internal and external conditions that allow good things, fun things, expansive things to take root. Awesome shows up when we say yes more often and say no to the things that sabotage our growth.

FEELING THE UPSET AND ALLOWING THE AWESOME IN THE SAME MOMENT

If you want to live an awesome life, you've got to act. Awesome doesn't sidle up when you are sitting on the couch. You've got to surround yourself with an atmosphere of awesome.

Too often, we forget to steep ourselves in the things that will infuse our life with spirit and energy and fun. We forget to look for the beauty. We lose our shot at awesome moments and awesome experiences when we become triggered by the guy who leaves the

Christmas lights up until May or the next-door neighbor who fires up his Harley at 6:00 a.m. We let ourselves become consumed by the irritation. We become grumbly, and then we find more things to make us grumbly.

I'm not saying *not* to get grumbly. I have mega grumbly days. I'm not saying to suppress anything. What I am saying is to allow yourself to feel it *all* instead of getting trapped in any one feeling.

When things start off rocky in the morning, then, with an unfortunate episode of exploding yogurt and a two-year-old's tantrum, you don't toss the whole day. You can't be having a bad day when you are only an hour into it. A couple of challenging incidents do not have to ruin it all. You can recognize each moment for what it is and be done, and then allow for the day to also be filled with opportunity for goodness. It can be there too.

My daughter—it's a no-school day—has been in my office 23.5 times in the last twenty-five minutes. Once, she started but didn't make it past the threshold because of the I-will-pluck-your-eyeballs-out-like-a-raven-if-you-take-one-more-step look I gave her.

She is cold and doesn't want to practice piano and she's hungry but we have nothing to eat and she wants to read but not one of the two hundred books we have in the house apparently strikes her fancy and it would all be better if I let her watch television and I just don't understand.

She is so stuck in the quicksand of complaining that she can't see the options in front of her. It's bringing her (and me, let me tell ya) down. That kind of complaining is like a dam stopping the flow of awesome. You can be grumpy and have moments of upset, but don't forget that awesome can exist right then too.

Retain the knowledge that even in a day laden with challenge, you can still go looking for a stunning sunset, or a sweet sip of good wine, or a hearty laugh with a special friend.

....

IN THE MOMENT PRACTICE:
SEE THREE

Next time you are stuck in upset, no matter how big or small, set a timer. Feel the upset. Ruminate. Complain for five or ten minutes. Then, at the end of that time, take a deep breath and look for three pieces of goodness. Three things that are right with the world. Start small if you have to, with things such as the breath in your body— but find those things. Notice how they exist even in the moments of upset.

....

RESPOND RATHER THAN REACT

How do you do it, though? How, in the middle of upset, can you swing this bus around and head for a better-feeling, positive land-scape?

It starts with being diligent in your response to both internal and external experiences and thought patterns.

I'm working on this. Believe me. This is where a giant sinkhole appears in my road to awesome and threatens to pull me in.

Say, for example, your partner walks in after a day at work—a whole eight hours away, including full-on lunch breaks— and your kid is lying on the ground bawling and your pasta is boiling over and you haven't showered and now that you think of it, you haven't even had lunch, and your beloved gives you a kiss hello and says, "Hi, what was your day like?"

And you look around at the wreckage while wiping up starchy pasta water and you begin twitching a little and you say, loudly, to be heard over the screeching kid:

"What do *you* think my day has been like?"

When we react like that—when we go with the unconscious emotional reaction triggered by external circumstances—everybody is going to feel a little bit beat up in the end. It's tough to get our mojo back after these kinds of episodes.

When we learn to respond—to consciously choose a deliberate and appropriate response—our concerns and frustrations are more likely to be heard and acted on, plus there can be a coming together, a solution-based connection that actually leads to compassion and understanding. When that happens, you are still in the atmosphere of awesome, and it's likely to circle around and catch up to you a lot faster.

This is what I'm after.

Reactions are usually emotional and laden with hostility and contempt, and sometimes victimhood. We speak in absolutes: "you never," "you always." We become inflated with the emotion.

We often react emotionally and unconsciously when we feel disrespected or threatened. We feel hurt, so we strike back with our words and behaviors.

It's like touching a hot burner. It happens so quickly that we don't realize until moments or hours or days later how much damage was done.

Reaction doesn't solve anything. In fact, our true needs often go unmet because we've added such drama to the situation. When you react, many times you then have to go back and fix, mop up, and apologize for the damage you have done with your bad behavior. You probably did have a valid point, somewhere along the way, but the true message of hurt or fear or inadequacy gets overlooked when we erupt with a geyser of emotion.

When we respond, we are conscious. We slow down. Articulate our thoughts. Choose our behavior. You can still be mad, if it serves you. You can still express your hurt and choose an appropriate response instead of a fly-off-the-handle reaction. This gives you power. You will be heard. You can then create a better or more illuminating experience, and that's the kind of atmosphere awesome thrives in.

....

Live Well: *Feel yourself slipping into a reactive mode? Go wash your hands. Often, it's the little behaviors and actions that can interrupt the negative thought pattern that leads us toward bad behavior—like snarky and sarcastic comebacks.*

Washing your hands can help you recover after a failure and promote greater feelings of optimism and calm, according to researchers at the University of Cologne. Hand-washing also eases stress after a hard decision.

So next time you are feeling uptight, defensive, or filled with negative feelings, go mindfully wash your hands and wash away the emotional ick.

....

Here's how it works. Your husband calls about fifteen minutes after he is expected home on a night when you planned to meet the girls for happy hour.

You react: "We talked about this; this is the night I'm going out with the girls. I told you about this three times. Do you ever remember anything? You always think of yourself first; it's always about you. This is just one more example of you not giving a rip about your family."

Or you respond: Deep breath, silent scream; then, with the desire for peace and resolution, you deliberately, consciously choose your behaviors and actions. Compassion is always a good lead-in.

"Wow, sounds like you have a lot going on. Must be challenging when the boss gives you more to do at the end of the day. Remember, tonight is the night I'm going out with the girls, so how can we figure this out?"

First off, this just feels better. Secondly, it gets you toward the solution you want—time with your friends. Finally, responding this way allows you to express yourself and be heard while building connection with your husband. It promotes conversation and compassion and understanding, and in the end, that goes a long way toward improving the other things that can threaten a relationship.

This makes sense, doesn't it? Be deliberate, be heard, work with compassion to solve the problem instead of adding to it. Then it might stop coming up time and time again.

> **Power Up:** While most everything is outside of our control, we can always choose how to respond. You can transcend the trouble or stay in the hostility, frustration, and anger. It's up to you to create the atmosphere of awesome.

STEPS TO AVOID THE ADULT MELTDOWN

In my family we talk in terms of meltdowns. I have a seven-year-old, and anyone with kids knows there are degrees of meltdowns from easy to explosive. I have 'em too. The other night I left the kale in the oven because I was on the verge of complete combustion in the kitchen. I went to my bedroom for a time-out. The kale burned, but it was the only casualty.

When we choose to respond rather than react, we increase our chances of maintaining a Meltdown-Free Zone. Here's how to do it.

1. **Take a deep breath.** Take another. This cannot be overstated. It is the simplest self-help tip out there. It forces you to pause, and it pushes oxygen into your brain and throughout your body to help ease stress. This deliberate breathing also helps you become conscious and mindful of the moment. All good things when you are looking for a suitable response instead of a fiery reaction.

2. **Ask the question.** If something triggers your angst or anger, clarify the situation. "What did you mean when you said I looked like a baboon?" Or "What was going

on for you when you forgot our appointment?"

Er, I wouldn't recommend anything sassy here, though—just get the info you need to foster understanding.

3. **Take it in.** Before you do anything else, observe the circumstances. The thing that triggered you is probably resolved by now. If it's not, you need to take an assessment before you come at it from a crazy-making place. Get out of your head and tune into your environment. Notice what is really happening now.

4. **Express, solve, repair, listen.** The Dalai Lama says that dialogue is the way to peace. If you can talk about your experience, give it a go. This is where I'll say, "I'm feeling really stressed because I didn't hear from you" or "I was hurt that I didn't receive your support." Express yourself and listen to the feedback. This isn't a time to attack but to explain.

5. **Get outta there.** Sometimes the best way to salvage a situation is to get out of Dodge. Slip away for a time-out. Get outta there. In this case, I will tell my family, usually in a very dramatic way, that I need to go and calm down for a minute, but that I will return. I head to the back bedroom and gulp down big breaths of air.

During this time-out, you can move further into reaction by thinking about all of the bad stuff he's done, or how life is so unfair, or what might happen. Or you can consider your next response by focusing on what you want, how to repair, and how to get back to the calm, compassionate place where awesome resides. Then you return a little saner, a little kinder.

....

PERENNIAL PRACTICE:
KNOWING YOUR TRIGGERS

There are things that set me off—assumptions, insensitivity, lack of effort, excuses. Those things just bug me. Knowing this about myself has helped me find some peace. It's helped me to understand myself better and respond with greater tolerance and calm when those things come up.

When someone or something sets you off, the problem is never outside of you. It is never the fault of another; it is all about your inner experience and how you choose to respond or react. Explore how you handle conflict and you'll be able to choose deliberate action to offset it. Here's how to do it.

1. Write down three challenges that you've faced in your life. What was going on when you felt upset? What triggered the emotions? Don't worry about complete sentences, just list your thoughts.

2. Look for a pattern. Do you see any common denominators? Perhaps each situation was marked by an interruption or an insult or lack of sleep. Remember, you are a common denominator too, because it's likely you were part of each circumstance.

3. Now consider the time when these patterns, these circumstances, are most likely to come up again. For me, it's around the dinner hour. Everyone is tired at the end of the day, everyone is hungry and short-tempered, everyone has needs, and mine are often the last to be met. Those conditions can trigger me if I'm not aware and choosing deliberate actions. Identify your prime trigger times. Notice when they show up in your day or life.

4. Develop a coping strategy. This stuff is going to come down, and how you respond will be the difference maker, so develop a plan right now for what you'll do next time so you can consciously respond and transcend the moment.

....

....

Be Awesome: *Sometimes our own awesomeness seems fleeting. We feel a separation between who we know ourselves to be—rational, compassionate, loving, intelligent—and the way we are behaving—like a raving lunatic. This is when it's time to connect with the elements. Take off your shoes and walk in the grass, or squish your feet in the mud, or wiggle your toes in the sand, or wade into the edge of a pond. Feel the heat radiating off the cement, the smoothness of the wood floor. Ground yourself physically by reconnecting with the elements of the earth and the Universe, the same elements that you are made up of, and you will reconnect with the awesome inside.*

....

CREATING THE CONDITIONS FOR AWESOME

Of course, some days it's easier to do this than others. Today, the sun is shining, a check came in the mail, and I know what I'm cooking for dinner. Smooth sailing. External events and conditions certainly influence our moods—often unconsciously. But taking awesome back is about managing our moments in a way that allows the good to show up no matter what's going on. Awesome then becomes a condition of our living.

There are things you can do to make this easier. Call them spiritual practices, self-help strategies, or Things to Keep Me from Losing My Mind, I don't care. But I think they are worth doing because when we are feeling good, we are also building our own resilience.

Think of it like a little spiritual lasagna. Layers of noodles and sauce and spices and cheese that takes about six years to prepare only to be eaten in about thirty seconds.

But with each layer, you get a little more goodness. The cheese is fine, but the cheese and the noodles and the sauce, now, that's just awesome.

Each time you lay down one of these practices, you are building a layer of something bigger, and unlike lasagna, the foundation you lay stays in place. It's there to help you create layers of awesome that make life more satisfying.

Power Up: With more laughter, practices and habits that open us to new experiences, and a playful spirit, we are apt to draw more of the good things into our lives.

Here is the framework for creating an awesome atmosphere every day.

Act with empathy. Lead with it. Slow down long enough to notice the experiences of others. Empathy breaches loneliness and builds connection. When someone you love hurts, you will hurt too. When you act with kindness, both of you will feel better.

Try something new. Look for novelty in your life. Do something different every day. Commit to bringing something new into your life, driving to a new place, reading a book from a genre you wouldn't ordinarily pick up, or listening to music you've never listened to before. The most powerful act of novelty is when I ask my husband a question about something I think I know. We've known each other for fifteen years and we are pretty familiar with each other, but when I take time to ask him a big, deep question, I'm always surprised by what he says. I love that. There is an intimacy and wonderment that is sweet and interesting when that happens. I have to work at this novelty stuff. I like my routine and I'm mired in my work and family. But on the days when I sit in a different chair in the family room, or eat at a new restaurant, or try a different workout routine, I feel energized. Novelty fuels curiosity. Curiosity feeds growth and meaning and fun.

Seek out humor. It isn't enough to have a laugh every once in a while. Go after the laughs in life. Watch a funny cat video. Play silly games with your kid. Read the comics or watch a comedy. Go after it and bring it in. Scores of studies show that laughter decreases the amount of stress hormones like cortisol and epinephrine that, in long sustained doses, can weaken our immune function. Laughter bolsters our immune system, improves blood pressure and blood sugar levels, and can even be a form of cardio exercise.

Play hard, have fun. You see how all this ties together? Try something new, laugh a lot, have more fun. Really, we are a culture of good workers. We get stuff done. But often our to-do list doesn't include anything fun.

Fun, play, humor—these things can actually help us be more productive, because we lighten up a bit, get sick less (fewer sick days means more time in the office), and connect to others in a way that enhances mental health and happiness.

Play also boosts vitality, fosters optimism, and prompts novelty. This is not a wasteful time suck. It's essential to our evolution and overall awesomeness.

It is also a state of being. Play is anything that is "purposeless, fun and pleasurable," says psychiatrist and play expert Stuart Brown. It's mostly about the experience, not about a prescribed outcome or goal. And it is personal.

My friend loves to play tennis; for me it's fun to read a mystery. I love dinners out with friends too. A hike can be play; so can time at the spa. Find what works for you and have more fun.

....

IN THE MOMENT PRACTICE:
PLANNING TO PLAY

Okay, all of this is well and good, but if you are a grown-up, paying the bills, managing relationships, and showing up at work every day, you may have forgotten what it feels like to play. Bringing playtime back into your life is critical to creating an atmosphere of awesome. Here's one way to do it.

1. Get quiet and take two minutes to think about the last time you really had fun. What were you doing? Write it down.

2. Then, consider something you'd really like to try, something you want to learn. Maybe you'd like to knit, or you are ready to take on the ukulele, or you'd like to go on an African safari. Write it down.

3. Finally, think about an activity that you enjoy every day—or something you'd like to enjoy every day. Maybe you love having lunch by the shore, or golfing with buddies, or working on your book. Write it down.

Now you have three things that might be fun for you. Do one today and every day. Mark it on your calendar, save time for it, carry it out. Plan to do one next week—enroll in the class or schedule the dinner date or start researching the trip. Make play a part of your life.

....

Often, there is a disconnect between what we think and what we feel and desire. There is a gap between the things that inspire and excite us and the things we do every day. Play can bring those pieces back together. There is time for both work and play, and the two support each other. We become more relaxed and focused when we are also having a little fun.

Indulge in daydreaming. Well, if you had problems with the point about play, this one might catch you up, because here I am advocating that you not only have fun, but that you then let your mind wander.

Pioneering psychologist Jerome Singer began exploring the phenomenon fifty years ago and found that almost everybody daydreams and that for most of us, daydreaming is a healthy function of our minds. Called mind wandering by fancier folk, daydreaming is "characterized by playful, wishful imagery and planful, creative thought," Singer says.

Daydreaming gives us the capacity to overcome constraints in the mind. We can solve problems, tap into memories, play with fantasies, create our futures, visualize vacations, and work through things in our dreams, says Scott Barry Kaufman. Those same daydreams that allow us to explore ideas, feelings, and sensations can even contribute to our happiness and other positive qualities.

So let your mind go for a few minutes. Paint a picture of where you'd like to be in the future. Reflect on the past. Create vivid scenes in your mind's eye. Those daydreams might just be the link to future awesome.

BUILDING AWESOME COMMUNITIES

All of this is better shared, of course. Awesome only gets bigger, stronger, more awesome when we come together. When we can experience these big moments with others, they can linger in our lives forever. When we come together with open minds and a willingness to explore and understand and learn, awesome takes on exponential power.

We then create an atmosphere where innovation is rampant, because we are more focused on the ideas rather than their imperfections. We teach others and we listen too, and we create space for everyone to get involved. We all become part of the larger experience, giving ourselves in whatever way we can contribute.

We work hard, give our best effort, and we continue—despite challenges—because we are part of a group that believes awesome is possible.

Think flash mobs, or public art displays, or the team of volunteers that puts together the school carnival or installs a new playground or cleans up the beaches. Think building a new business with a team of employees, or producing a high school musical, or nurturing a community garden, or working with your family to host a garage sale or throw a party or even clean up afterward.

When we come together with a sense of collaboration, in the spirit of contribution and appreciation, the atmosphere becomes supercharged for awesome. It's inspiring and fun and life-changing for all.

....

Night Cap: *As you unwind from the day or drift off to sleep, take a deep breath, relax your body, and let yourself daydream. Imagine that you are living your best life five years from now. You have an abundance of love and good health and money and passion and purpose. What does that look like? Dream big in vivid colors and bold images and just let your mind go.*

....

ONE PATH: CREATING COMMUNITY AND ART

Larry Moss is an artist, but when he works he's creating more than the illustrations he draws or the photographs he snaps. He's creating more than the gigantic acrocanthosaurus or the ten-thousand-square-foot haunted house that he and others shaped entirely out of latex balloons.

What Larry Moss is creating is community.

He's known for his elaborate and intricate balloon sculptures, but he also sees his work as a way to access the gifts and talents of others by collaborating with them to create art.

"I don't think I can grow or evolve as a person or an artist if I don't pay attention to other ideas or work with other people to share and teach and try things," Moss says. "Also, how can they appreciate my art if they haven't had their own experience with it? It builds appreciation."

The idea of creating community through massive balloon sculptures took hold nearly two decades ago when Moss was invited to Japan to work with a team of people to construct a parade float.

Moss didn't speak Japanese and most on the team didn't speak English, nor had they worked with balloons before. Yet somehow the group bonded and was able to complete the task. The experience inspired Moss to create other large-scale community art installations.

Though he does create other work on his own in the quiet of his Rochester, New York, art studio, the "fine art of folding air," as Moss describes it, has always been a powerful way for Moss to build connection with others.

He first started honing his talent as a high school kid riding on New York subways. He practiced making small balloon sculptures while riding the train to and from school. Moss worked his way through college as a street magician and balloon sculptor who also performed at children's birthday parties and other events. After graduating with degrees in applied math and computer science, Moss went to work as a computer programmer. But he felt trapped and isolated by the office job. He returned to school for a degree in elementary school education, but realized that his "air-bending art" had paid for his education and could be a full-time job. He now operates Airigami with his partner and fiancée, artist Kelly Cheatle.

"I like exposing people to new experiences, and that is certainly an aspect of education," Moss says. "But what I mostly like is finding new ways to connect people with art. These large projects are about creating an accessible experience. It's about putting art in people's hands so they can create it too."

That means getting to know others and playing to their strengths. On the larger projects, Moss works with a team of artists and volunteers who tie and bend balloons. Others contribute design ideas, still others build structures, and some people volunteer to help with whatever needs to be done, like picking up lunch for the crew. There is a place for everyone, a chance for everyone to be involved if they desire, and that's what makes the experience so powerful, Moss says.

"There is no limit to the contributions that can be made through art. I'm having a blast and other people have fun with it too. I never know what is going to come next and the more I do with others, the more that I want to do. People can contribute in so many different ways. So far I haven't found anyone who can't create at all. It is the connection with others that is most important, not the mechanics of what we are doing or what we are creating."

CHAPTER 11

THE AWESOME UNCERTAINTY

■ ■ ■

> *The quest for certainty blocks the search for meaning.*
> *Uncertainty is the very condition to impel man to unfold*
> *his powers.*
>
> **—ERICH FROMM**

Not long before my grandmother died, she asked my father, "Am I dying?" She'd stopped eating. Her lungs were filling with fluid, and at ninety-three her body and brain were wearing out. Hospice was helping and the nurse had predicted she had a few days left. Family members had gathered.

"Yes," my father said, "I think you are. How do you feel about that?"

"Well, I don't know," she said. "I've never done it before." Then she smiled a bit, chuckled at the humor. Shrugged at the truth.

There is so much we don't know about death—and about life. There is so much we can't possibly know. And I'm glad for it.

Not saying it's always comfortable, this unknowing which pervades everything. I'd like to know that my investments are a sure thing and my body will hold out for years to come. I'd like to know that my kid will grow up and be safe and healthy and wealthy enough to support me in my retirement (right now her plans are to live in a mansion with a log ride out back, so things are looking good). Heck, I'd like to know what I should cook for dinner tomorrow—it's the little things, people.

But life is best lived on a need-to-know basis. It's the mystery, the ever-lingering uncertainty about what will turn up in our day that keeps us learning, growing, curious, alive. Nothing is ever stagnant, and that is so reassuring because it means we will not be stuck in the trouble spots. If nothing is fixed, if particulate matter is swirling and vibrating around us, that means that even the tough times won't last forever. It also means that awesome can exist in every moment.

But that same awesome cannot exist without uncertainty and change. Remember, by definition, awe is vast and it requires accommodation. We must actually adjust, adapt, change our view, our feelings, our thoughts to process anything that is truly awesome. Awe changes us.

Uncertainty is our greatest ally, then, when it comes to building an awesome life. For most of us, uncertainty is also numero uno on the list of things that stress us out.

We need to get over it. Make peace with it. Find a way to shrug into the end, like my grandmother did, to smile a bit and say, "Well, I don't know; I've never done it before." Then open to the adventure ahead.

Power Up: The awesome in our lives will be limited until we can also embrace the positive qualities of uncertainty and change. Awesome, by its very nature, requires us to adapt and accommodate. To have awesome lives, then, we must grow comfortable with change.

LIVING WITH COSMIC UNCERTAINTY

For me, this whole idea of making peace with the uncertainty of life is so much easier than my previous modus operandi, which was to fight any change in my schedule and get really snappy and uptight trying to control every little thing.

When I learned how to let up a bit—cancer and the kid taught me a few lessons—when I learned to let go of the things that I cannot control and to mind my own business on just about everything else, a surprising thing happened: My life still worked. In fact, it was better, smoother, more fun.

When I'm able to let go, I am better able to tap into the energy of intuition and flow, and then life becomes dynamic. It expands and constricts in all the right places. It was a tremendous relief to discover that I don't have to know everything and do everything for my life to work out.

It is scary to think that it all comes down to us. That if we can't navigate through change and uncertainty, it will all just fall apart. Nope. Wrong. Here's the deal: You don't have to know what the heck you are doing. Just show up, become conscious and curious, and take inspired, compassionate actions, and you will learn what you need as you need it. This is a leap of faith for sure, but it works. Every time.

Look, if I can barely figure out the television remote, imagine how crazy the Universe would be if I had to manage something like say, the law of gravity. But it all works without my meddling. When you welcome the uncertainty of life rather than resisting the inevitable, life becomes softer, expansive.

You start living well with what is, instead of worrying about what might be. And as you relax into knowing that you can adapt and roll with the tough stuff that comes your way, you are also able to expand and see the beauty and goodness that rolls in too. You become capable of both adapting to change and creating it. This means you can go from unhappiness to joy, from loneliness to love. Those are a couple of the possibilities that change allows.

Life, then, becomes infused with opportunity and the possibility of everything.

TURNING UNCERTAINTY AROUND

Course, even knowing this, few of us welcome uncertainty and change. We give it dirty looks when we think no one's watching. We mock it; we complain about it. We loathe it. We buzz about all the scary changes when a new boss walks in, though the old one was a tyrant. We stress about new schools and neighborhoods and technology. We even get uptight over new hairdos if they are too different from what we are used to. New hairdos, people! We've got to get over this.

I know many people are even reluctant to try new foods or travel to new places because they aren't sure how the experience will play out. Can you imagine living in a world with only vanilla ice cream because you were too uncertain to try the chocolate or the lemon gelato?

To have the lemon gelato, to have the awesome in your life, you've got to embrace the uncertainty. You've got to move away from the vanilla that you know (tasty in its own right) for the possibility of something new, unique, interesting. This requires a new mindset and a slew of new habits.

The fastest way to shift toward the good stuff and neutralize our fears of uncertainty is to step into the present moment. Move into now. Just like teacher Eckhart Tolle says, there is no pain in the present, no pain in the now. It is only our projection of what might happen in the future that causes our stress. Remain present and you will remain with awesome.

....

IN THE MOMENT PRACTICE:
SLIP INTO THE MOMENT

Feel yourself teetering on the edge of drama and worry about what might be? Stop, take a deep breath, and, as you slowly exhale, imagine the worry slipping out and freeing you up to be present to what is right now.

Then, use all your senses to root you in the present. Notice the sounds in the room, the feeling of the air moving into and out of your body as you continue to take deep breaths. Look around and focus on what you are seeing and smelling. Keep up the slow and deep breathing until the worries have slipped out and been replaced by the peace of the present moment.

....

Here's how it works. Next time you are faced with a big change or a degree of uncertainty—say, you're headed to a new doctor and worried about what she might find—turn it around. You can dwell on the possibility of high cholesterol or extra pounds or high glucose—none of which are known, none of which are helpful thoughts—or you can simply focus on the present and celebrate that you are making healthy choices by getting some baseline information with a new doc.

You may eventually discover that you need to change your diet or get more exercise. You may also discover that your cholesterol is low and your weight is fine. Or you might learn that this particular doctor has Jolly Rancher candies in the reception candy dish. Life and the experiences within it offer up an abundance of possibilities, so why then do we choose to dwell on the ones that freak us out?

Do it differently. Instead of dwelling on the drama, shift your perspective to the present or the positive. From there, peace is possible.

WHAT IF OR WHY NOT?

Often, when the vibration of change moves into our lives, filling us with feelings of uncertainty, we fall into our negativity bias. We are, after all, highly imaginative creatures who have become very good at creating scary stories about all the troubles that could befall us. Then we go on the Internet to confirm that, yes, our fears are justified. You wanna be scared out of your head? Start looking up photos on the Internet.

But if you want to feel energized by the other possibilities that are also out there, those that are accessible and existing right now in the same moment, shut off the Internet, reframe the uncertainty, and stop feeding the fear. You can do this by asking "Why not?" instead of "What if?"

You know how this works: Someone urges you to apply for the job and your inner curmudgeon chimes in with "What if I don't get it?" Or you decide to get married and you hear "What if the marriage fails?" Or maybe you're what-iffing your health: "What if I get cancer?" "What if I get that flu going around and miss the meeting?" What if?

When we what-if our life away, we get locked into worry, fear kicks in, and we start ruminating over things that haven't even happened yet and probably never will. *I better be prepared just the same,* we think. We build an emotional bunker and hunker down against the evils that could strike at any moment, and we stop participating in life. We become blind to our own power and resilience, blocked from the love and joy and peace that also exist in every moment. We fail to act with compassion, because what if we do and we get hurt? We don't try for the promotion, because what if we can't do the job? We don't get that check-up, because what if they find something?

See how silly this is? You don't even know the job description and yet you've decided to give up on the promotion.

Instead of "What if?", say "Why not?" and have a little faith that you will learn what you need to know to prevail. Why not try for the job? If you get it, you will have the information you need then to decide whether or not to accept it. Why not go on the date? Could be your soul mate, or at least a free meal. Why not go to the doc to find out that you are perfectly healthy?

"What if I buy these cute size-eight jeans and then gain weight?" becomes "Why not buy these cute new jeans?"

"What if I marry this guy and we end up getting divorced?" becomes "Why not allow myself to love and trust that we will love well together?"

"What if the cancer comes back?" becomes "Why not live every moment the best I can?"

With *what if,* you are avoiding and resisting. *Why not* invokes wonder, action, creativity.

....

Be Awesome: *Awe is often a result of awareness and conscious thinking; despair is not. So let go of the thoughts that drag you down. You can consciously choose thoughts that increase good feelings. It doesn't mean that you are denying the negatives; it means only that you are putting your focus on the other possibilities that exist in that same moment. Right now, notice something you haven't noticed before, or find something unexpected in the familiar, and you will know that awesome is always there even if you don't immediately see it.*

....

UNCORK YOUR COMMON SENSE, LIVE WITH RIGHT ACTION

When you shift your perspective and ask *why not* instead of *what if,* you see things with a little more clarity. That makes sense, right? It's more efficient to look at all sides of a situation before reacting, instead of reacting emotionally from fear or choosing a course of action that leads away from your authentic self.

This is where common sense kicks in. What feels right, what makes sense according to your values, is often the best move.

Of course we override this sense. We look to the Internet or friends or books for answers or guidance on big decisions. We let external forces direct us. But often the best answers lie within us. They bubble up from our life experience and knowledge and compassion and faith, creating for us a bedrock of wisdom that can guide us through any uncertainty, or at least give us the optimism that we can survive it.

Sure, you can go out and gather the skills and info you need to cope with the day-to-day stuff—it's very helpful to know how to sew a button and fold clothes. You should seek knowledge. But don't discard what you already know, the common sense that is your internal compass. It will also guide you to the next step. Use it to recognize your own distinct capabilities.

FIVE RULES TO HELP COPE WITH UNCERTAINTY

1. **If it doesn't fit, don't force it.** Sometimes even the things we think we want most of all aren't a good fit for our values, needs, or health. Sometimes uncertainty along the path is there to show us that we need to change course.

2. **Play nice with others.** Your fears and funky mood don't give you the right to treat others poorly. We need each other. Your success impacts my success. Your joys fuel mine. When you are facing change, you will be strengthened by the support, humor, and kindness of others. Offer the same.

3. **Do your best, even if it's crap.** Sometimes it will be. Seriously. When you are doing something new, when you are moving through an uncertain time, you will be called on to do things and tap skills you aren't all that familiar with. Do your best anyhow. Don't make excuses. Show up and give it your all. Sometimes even your best effort won't be so hot. But you will learn and get better. It is so much easier to live with the crap when you know you gave it your all.

4. **Be polite.** Show respect to others, to the circumstances, to yourself by being a good sport, saying "Thank you," looking others in the eye. Hold the door open. Not only does it make the day smoother when we look out for each other this way, it also fosters connection and love and cooperation, and all that can yield the next bit of information you'll need to deal with changing circumstances.

5. **Do the right thing when no one is looking.** If you do nothing else, do this. Don't look for praise or reward—this is about self-respect. About being true to yourself. Connecting to your essence. Do the right thing because you are a higher energy and an authentic person of integrity. When the world is ever-changing and you feel afraid and slightly unhinged, the one thing you have, for sure, is you and all that you are. You are an awesome force. You alone can change the world. I'm not overstating this. That is the fortitude of your authentic power. But to access it, to recognize all that, you've got to be true no matter who is in the room. It is the one thing you can count on. Don't betray yourself.

Buddhists talk of "right action." It is the fourth element of the Noble Eightfold Path to enlightenment, and it speaks to the ethical conduct of the followers.

I think of it as good behavior. Don't hurt others. Don't take from others. Don't abuse or physically harm yourself or others. Do not abuse drugs or alcohol, or other "sensual pleasures." Don't sleep with another's partner. Don't be stupid—okay, so the Buddhists don't actually say that last one, but I think it applies. Live with compassion and these tips will support you no matter the uncertainties you face.

GROWTH THROUGH KINDNESS

The other stabilizing force that will help you roll with the waves of uncertainty and change rather than being swept away by them is kindness.

When we are stressed, trying to figure it all out and ramping up our skills to deal with the diagnosis or new job or baby or vacation or new house or shifting beliefs or any of the other conditions that can keep us awake at night, we become really self-absorbed. Me, me, me. *How will this affect me? How hard will this be for me to manage? Who will help me? What will I do?*

This self-centered focus can easily ensnare us in rumination and isolation. When we are feeling tested, we tend to think we are the only ones. Yet even as you deal with your changes, others around you are dealing with theirs. And kindness can free you from your own stuck cycle while helping them through theirs.

Power Up: When we are afraid of change or uncertainty, self-absorption and isolation take hold. Kindness moves us to a more open state. From here, we can shift among the more positive perspectives to actually cope better with whatever we are facing. This is when we can also be a beacon of light for others.

Spiritual psychologist Milan Ljubincic says that kindness is the way for all of us to grow and evolve.

"We must be more discerning about the truth," he says. "And the truth is that everything is interconnected, the beauty is when we connect with our core self. We can do that with compassion."

THRIVE WITH CHANGE

Alright, so you got this: Change is a part of life, and you can discover great possibilities for growth and opportunity when you embrace that uncertainty. You can thrive not despite, but because of what comes into your experience.

Some of the most meaningful and grand experiences of my life have come when I've felt most out of sorts, when I moved into unfamiliar territory and expanded into the uncertainty. There is meaning there for you too, in every circumstance.

THREE QUICKIES TO HELP YOU THRIVE IN UNCERTAIN TIMES

1. **Study the lesson.** Look for the teachable moment and then do the learning. Every situation has something to show us. Discover what it is. Learn about yourself and your tenacity. Get information about whatever you are facing. Explore your emotions, your spirituality, your beliefs. Study and learn about your relationship. If you hate your job, don't just see that as your challenge; learn about the specific aspects of the job that you dislike. Use the time of uncertainty to teach you, and instead of being scary, it becomes interesting.

2. **Watch your language.** Listen to those inner and outer voices and be careful what you say. Never, ever speak in

absolutes. Use language that reminds you of your skill and capability rather than your failures.

3. **Rest.** Just go to bed. Change can wear us out. Sleep is restorative. It also helps our brains expand and grow and solve problems—all of which are pluses when we are moving through a new or daunting experience. Make time for sleep. Use it to buffer your physical body and gain clarity and you will thrive.

THREE WAYS TO ACTIVATE YOUR AWESOME

When you get used to this idea of uncertainty as a positive and dynamic element of an awesome life consciously lived, you begin to thrive. Then you can make something out of all of this positive energy. It attracts innovation and creation, contribution and connection. Soon, you'll begin to fly rather than just getting by.

Here's how it works. You have a new baby and you're thrown into the spin cycle of life. You are filled with uncertainty and having a hard time coping with the changes that come from living with a person who needs to eat every fifteen minutes—and that's just you. The baby is eating a bunch too. But that gets you thinking.

"Huh, if I'm having a hard time—if I no longer have the energy or time to meditate and take care of my mental, emotional, and spiritual self—I imagine other mothers are constrained the same way."

It was exactly that thought that led me to write my first book, *Imperfect Spirituality.*

One of the most uncertain, change-filled times in my life became one of the most creative, exciting, awesome times both personally and professionally.

Here are a few other tips that can help you activate your awesome:

Meditation

Don't let the word get you all hot and bothered. I'm simply talking about settling down, getting quiet, and putting focused attention on your thoughts. Do this for five minutes a day. More is even better, but you are not a loser if you don't meditate longer. Meditation heightens your powers of concentration and attention. It also improves clarity, calm, and energy. It can help you move into the present moment, ease stress and pain, and help you feel restored.

 Tip: Don't judge your thoughts or worry that you are doing this wrong. Believe me; your mind will be busy at times. Simply notice those thoughts, imagine yourself blowing them away with your next breath, and then return your focus to your breath, or a mantra, if you like.

Self-compassion

When we treat ourselves kindly even after a mistake, we are more likely to try again. Research by developmental psychologist Kristin Neff and others also shows that self-compassion makes us more accountable and productive. This means we have a greater shot at accomplishing our goals. When you are dealing with new circumstances brought about by changing conditions, you are bound to make mistakes. Next time, treat yourself gently, and you'll make good from the bad.

But, how do you do this? How do you treat yourself more kindly even after you've screwed up? Start by acknowledging your blunder. Be accountable for it and apologize or repair it if you need to. Then identify what led to the error and give yourself a break. Say something like "Well, I blew it and I feel bad about that, but I've done my best to improve the situation and I'm human and people make mistakes. I'll work to do better next time." Then move on. Beating yourself up keeps you tight and unhappy. Self-compassion frees you up to find awesome ahead.

Imagination

Come on, even if you choose the red lipstick over the Pomegranate Promenade, you've still got imagination. And when you use it—or really just let it loose—it's a direct line to awesome.

Imagination is aliveness, says Ljubincic. "Creativity and imagination in my mind are so important because they help us on our journey. When you are living with a lack of interest, when you are coasting, you are not living."

Imagination is the thing that can help us tap into our purpose, appreciate the beauty in the stars, and create goals. It can inspire love, illuminate meaning, and offer up the possibility that everything can be okay again even when it seems everything is falling apart. All of that, the meaning of now and the possibility for the future, derive from our imagination.

This kind of creative energy is not only about creating a master work or writing a book, it is about creating a life. About living fully in the moments you have now. Those moments are accessible to all of us.

Imagination, Ljubincic says, is a practice, something that can be cultivated and learned. It shows up in the doing, not in thinking about the doing.

I once watched a cooking show where one of the contestants had to cook an entire meal without a pan or a pot. In twenty minutes she constructed cookery from tinfoil and stove burners and lids. It was fun to watch, and when she completed the challenge, her face was stretched wide with satisfaction. In twenty minutes, she did something she'd thought impossible just a few minutes before. Something that she drew from her imagination.

Tip: Deliberately access your imagination every day. Just as you sit down to a daily practice of meditation or make a regular trip to the gym, just as you nourish your body with regular meals, nourish your soul with your imagination.

Here are three ways to fire up your imagination:

Push your own boundaries. Challenge yourself to take on routine tasks differently. Each month, eat a meal at a different international restaurant and sample new cuisine. Use your non-dominant hand to cook, write, or brush your teeth. Novelty awakens our brains and gets our imaginations flowing.

Become a seeker. Our imagination is ignited by the questions we ask, not by the answers we find, Ljubincic says. Ask the big questions: *What is our purpose? What is all of this? What is the meaning of my life?*

"We don't always get the answers we want, but we will be guided to where we need to be through our inquiry," Ljubincic says.

Merge with awesome. Look up at the stars and contemplate the Universe. Lie down in a field of wildflowers, swing on the playground swings, participate in a flash mob dance, sit with an artist and watch him paint. Immerse yourself in beauty, lose yourself in the mystique of life, and steep in the insights of your own imagination.

"We don't need to know the step-by-step way to do any of this," Ljubincic says. "If we had all the answers then life would lose its mystique. Our creativity though, our imagination, taps us into where we want to go and lets us move into the experience which, then, taps into our hearts.

"We create our own meaning by the way we envision our own life. We don't need to know where we are going; the secret is simply to keep seeking because that is the true adventure."

....

IN THE MOMENT PRACTICE:
WRITE YOUR HERO'S TALE

Think about the changes and challenges you are facing and the uncertainty you feel.

Then, create your Hero's Tale.

Imagine that you are on an epic journey through this uncertainty. But you are energized. You have the strength, talents, skills, and superpowers to travel this road and live an awesome life.

Imagine the journey in vibrant detail. What are your skills and strengths? What adversity will you overcome? What gifts will you receive? How will it end? Will you save yourself and the world and leave something better in your wake?

Does this seem a bit cheesy? Totally! But it's also fun and surprisingly empowering. I've done this at various times as a way of coping with rheumatoid arthritis. I sure haven't loved every aspect of my experience with illness, but I haven't suffered with it either. It's simply been an experience, and I've used the biggest setbacks to create a new story of strength.

I have always emerged stronger, with a keen ability to contribute something positive to the world.

Now, go write your story. Play, daydream, imagine. Then go live it.

....

LIVING THE PEAK EXPERIENCE

The red number on the digital clock hanging on the hospital wall said 4:59 a.m. I remember the time. I remember every detail, really. My husband was snoring quietly, but snoring just the same, on the pull-out bed next to my hospital bed. Our daughter, born the day before, was in the nursery, so I could sleep a bit and gain strength after my C-section. I was hurting, but awake and thinking about her and my new family, and in the quiet, I was feeling so grateful that of all the things that could have gone wrong, nothing had.

Yet I was nervous too. How would I do all this? Loving and feeding and changing and showing up every day, always? How would I even know this little stranger I was soon to take home? Would we even recognize each other?

I felt inadequate and alone and so tired. Already so tired. Then, in the gray darkness permeated by the light leaking under the door from the hallway, I heard a cry. A rooster squawk, really. It wasn't loud. I could barely hear it over the hum of the machines in my room in the maternity ward. But, in that second, I knew it was Sweet P. I knew her instantly.

A second later the nurse came through the door.

"Your daughter was just asking for you," the nurse said. "So I thought I'd come in and see if you were awake."

And she laid Sweet P in my arms and I pulled that baby to my chest as though I'd always done it. As though we'd known each other forever.

The moment was life-changing. It was awesome. I think about it often, and each time, it fills me with emotion and promise and the knowledge that I am enough to handle whatever comes down.

WHAT IS A PEAK EXPERIENCE?

Peak experiences are transformative. They instill us with a greater sense of our capability and leave us with an expanded view of ourselves. When we have one of these experiences, we are forever changed by it.

In 1964, psychologist Abraham Maslow defined a peak experience as a moment of intense well-being that fills us with wonder and awe. It often feels like an awakening, an epiphany. One moment we were in the dark, and in the very next, we have a clearer sense of ourselves, an expanded view of our experience and purpose that often leads to transformation and change.

These moments—which can sometimes be sustained for weeks or even months if we are immersed in the pursuit of a specific and finite goal, like writing a book or training for a marathon, or if we are going through a time of transition such as retirement—often evolve out of a time of turmoil and can cause "quantum change," says psychological researcher William Miller.

The sudden realization or awareness—like my "I'd know her anywhere" understanding—often causes us to shift our values, change our behaviors, and organize our lives in a way that feels more authentic and more alive. We reorganize our priorities and act in new ways.

Here's how it works. You get diagnosed with cancer. During a chemotherapy treatment, you have this expanded awareness that the only thing that matters is your family. When you recover from the illness, you quit your job to become a stay-at-home dad.

While many associate peak experiences with climbing a mountain, meeting a goal, or other big-time events, they don't have to be showstoppers to make a profound difference.

Peak experiences can also come by way of subtle shifts and personal insights that appear when we are emerging from turmoil or having a moment of deep appreciation that comes when we are in a state of awe. This leads to alchemy. A blend of our dreams and desires and aspirations with an extraordinary moment of self-realization that transports us and awakens us to our authenticity and a life of deeper meaning and purpose.

I had a peak experience at 2:00 a.m. in a Reno bar with my eighty-three-year-old grandmother. Another when a friend and I came upon floating lanterns in a lake in a small village in the Alps. Another while writing my first book.

Peak experiences don't just belong to the special and wise—though we are all both of those things. Life, for all of us, is filled with extraordinary and intense moments. They are there for us, as Maslow said, these times of intense well-being that fill us with wonder and awe. When we are peaking, we aren't caring about what others think—yet at the same time, we are feeling more connected. We experience a oneness or nonduality.

Peak experiences also produce action. We move into this new sense of ourselves; we embrace the change and stand in awe of the remarkable moments that are our lives.

HOW TO PEAK?

When we put ourselves out there and engage in the world, we leave the door open for this kind of transcendent experience. Often, when we are living close to our passions and values, peak experiences show up spontaneously.

They come, too, when difficult situations require us to broaden our view of the world, when we are looking for answers, something to carry us through. But other peak experiences, scientists say, can be created through deliberate choice and behavior.

Much like the way we evoke inspiration or fire up our imaginations, creating peak experiences requires us to challenge ourselves, to create, to daydream about the future and reflect on the meaning of today.

We've got to move into the world, pursue our passions and dreams, live authentically, and participate. Altruism can also ignite these intense feelings.

When we are giving to others, we are on the edge of a peak experience. We are creating connection and fulfilling our needs for meaning and contribution. That changes how we experience the moment and ourselves.

Of course, peak experiences require us to get comfortable with uncertainty. To place ourselves into new situations, to engage despite the risk. And we never know when they are going to show up.

In this and other ways, uncertainty can shake you up or inspire you. Often we become derailed by change, but what if we shift perspective and recognize that only with uncertainty can there be growth, awe, and peak experience? Change allows us to love deeply when we hadn't loved before. To live our passions when we've only just discovered them. Change and uncertainty are the portal that allows us to expand into our awesome. Instead of viewing uncertainty and change, then, as madness, savor the mystery and the magic that they also instill.

....

PERENNIAL PRACTICE: TAKING ANOTHER PEAK

One of the most transformative aspects of peak experiences is that we never forget them. They are intense and detailed and etched in our memories for a lifetime. Though there can be a low that follows the peak, we can still draw from them throughout our lives and recapture their spirit to inform our moments today.

Do that now. Pull out a journal and pen. Reflect for five or ten minutes on a profoundly intense, life-changing moment or period of time. Think about the experience, the details of it, and the transformation or awakening that occurred.

Then tell a story about it on paper. Write about what happened and when and where. Don't worry about complete sentences or grammar, but do capture the emotion and intensity. Use strong details and verbs. Write it in present tense as if you were there again.

If you feel like it, share what you've written with another. Allow that person to be part of this life-changing moment. Reread your entry from time to time. It will remind you of who you are and what you are capable of, as well as of the change and uncertainties that are there to ramp up our lives rather than detract from them.

....

....

Night Cap: *Is the stress of change and uncertainty keeping you awake at night? Instead of what-iffing about what might happen, reflect on what has happened.*

Think back to a time where you felt filled with the angst of uncertainty and remember what came out of that time. A new job, a new house, perhaps a new relationship or a different take on the world?

Uncertainty often leads to creation and innovation. That is awesome. We need only to remember it's possible.

....

ONE PATH: GROWING FROM UNCERTAIN OPPORTUNITY

It was late one night in 2012 when Rory Rogan sat in his room at the United States Merchant Marine Academy sewing a simple backpack. He needed a bag to haul around his mountain climbing gear and decided to try creating his own. He had no idea the pack would launch a philanthropic corporation that now supports education in Africa.

But Rogan has always been one to find the opportunity within uncertainty.

Within months of sewing that first prototype in 2012, an idea began to take shape. What if he could use these bags not only to build a company, but to educate kids?

Rogan had learned about the African Education Program (AEP) in Zambia a year before. The group offers a safe haven for elementary and middle school students to study after school. It also provides them with a meal and encouragement from the staff. For many of the students who come from surrounding villages, this center is the only shot they will have at finishing school.

In Zambia, children are required to pay for their schooling after the seventh grade. Most cannot afford to continue. But with sponsors through centers like the AEP, some of these kids will graduate. And Rogan wanted to find a way to help make that happen. With a ticket he was given for graduation, he and his mom headed to Zambia to see the center firsthand.

Soon after, Rogan's backpack company took root. The company, known as "Be," began producing bags in New York City and began a movement to support future generations.

For every bag sold, ten dollars of the proceeds goes toward a child's education in Africa. Thirteen children received the gift of an education in the first year alone, and both the company and its philanthropy continue to grow. Each pack comes with a Hope Patch stitched inside. The patch includes an individual and unique message written by a child from Zambia.

Rogan isn't sure how big the company will get, or how it will develop, or even what's next, but he remains committed to two things: helping the kids and corporate transparency. Every Be patron can see exactly how their money is being used to help kids.

"I'm trying to live with gusto, to say 'Okay, I don't have to know what's going to happen here, but I am going to work with it,' and I am open and grateful for the opportunities that come my way and I'm just taking advantage of them all, the best I can," says Rogan.

"I couldn't tell you where this is going to lead. But, you know, it's okay that I don't know. I like to plan ahead but also like to respond to life to see where the options are."

CHAPTER 12

LIVING AN AWESOME LIFE

■ ■ ■

There is no passion to be found in playing small—in settling for a life that is less than the one you are capable of living.

—NELSON MANDELA

Above my desk, in the shelf of the computer hutch, there are three metal letters, each about four inches tall. Together they spell *AWE*. It took me a while to figure that out. They came in the bottom of a Christmas stocking. A gift from Santa Claus, I presume.

I pulled them out, laid them on the floor, spelled out *WAE*, and looked at them quizzically. Then *EWA*. What the heck? Finally, I saw the *AWE*. I'm quick like that.

Of course the *AWE* had been there all along, concealed only by my perspective and my thought patterns. That's often how it goes with the awe of our lives too. Our lives are always filled with elements of awe; we are surrounded by awesome, but we miss out when we are too busy to pay attention, or can't make the connection, or can't find the awe among the unconscious clutter of our lives. This leaves us with an empty, unsettled feeling, like we've forgotten something but we can't remember what.

My metal letters remind me to go looking, to seek out the awe in the world and in myself; they guide me to set the intention to live an awesome life.

SETTING THE INTENTION FOR AWESOME

To see and savor and create and appreciate the awe that threads through our lives, we must get after it. We must actively practice the things that will draw it into our conscious experience. This is where things get practical. We stop thinking and we start doing and being the things that illuminate the awesome. Here, we let the drama of life ease into acceptance and let the sadness be uplifted by the beauty and love that are there too.

This takes some effort, of course, some practice. We've got to replace the habits of judgment and worry that have kept us busy and separate from our higher self with those qualities that support expansion and clarity and peace and possibility. We must be deliberate in our approach to awe and become a conscious creator. We must intend it.

To shape your intention, consider which qualities, things, or energies you want to bring into your life.

Declare them aloud—in present tense—right now.

Take action right away toward your intention.

Pay attention as the manifestations of your intentions show up.

Master manifestors like Tony Burroughs and others also remind us that in order for our intentions to manifest, they must be for the highest good of all concerned, including you, and the Universe. Declare it.

You can ask for stuff too—a big-screen television, more money, pizza for dinner—and there is a likelihood that with your focus on these things, the circumstances and people you need to create these outcomes will show up in your life.

Here's how it works. I intended to secure a new client and boost my monthly income. With that clear focus in mind, I did things during my workday that helped me identify some opportunities I hadn't recognized before. I mentioned this effort to a friend, who suggested I call her contact, who just happened to be the editor of a publication I'd targeted. He was looking for someone to write just the kind of articles I write, and I landed a new assignment within a couple of hours.

But intention is so much bigger than jobs or money or other external rewards. It is a powerful life-builder. These days I set my focus not so much on the things I want, but on the experiences and qualities I want to attract. I use intention to help me hone my awareness and express my purpose and to keep from freaking out.

My intentions sound like this:

I intend to be focused and creative in my work today.

I intend to let things go.

I intend to see awe and opportunity in unexpected places throughout my day.

I intend to find humor and peace even during stressful times.

I intend to have productive and positive connections with the people I'm working with today.

With an intention in mind, you will begin attracting all kinds of awesome into your life. When you learn to savor it, the experience will also elevate you.

····················

IN THE MOMENT PRACTICE: INTENDING YOUR DAY

When you wake up in the morning, give gratitude for the day ahead. Then, sit on the edge of your bed and set the intention for your day. I think of it as a theme statement.

I will set other intentions before phone calls or meetings or writing sessions, but none is more powerful than the one I set in the morning. It keeps me focused on the things that matter most to me in that day and sets the tone for awe. For example:

I intend to experience good health and take care of my body.

I intend to move with peace and joy.

I intend to be loving and compassionate to all whom I encounter.

With your intention in mind, say it aloud.

Feel the emotion that will arrive with that intention.

Ask that the intention manifest if it is for your highest good and the highest good of others and the Universe.

Then start your day.

....

SAVORING LIFE

Savoring is the act of noticing the positive, amazing, awesome things in your life and then pausing to engage with the good feelings that come out of that, says Loyola University professor of psychology Fred Bryant, author of *Savoring: A New Model of Positive Experience.* It is the process of becoming aware of both the good things in life and your inner, personal experience of them. You might then express those good feelings through gratitude or other outlets, but savoring requires you first to identify the feeling in the moment. To be with it. Absorb it.

Its power lies in our ability to notice the little goodnesses that are part of our daily experience, instead of taking them for granted, Bryant says. Happiness and other positive experiences then arise from those goodnesses.

"It is in the slowing down that we are better able to notice the things that are there to savor. You want to stop and smell the roses? Well, you can't just roll your window down as you drive by the garden," Bryant says. "Getting more, moving faster is not better. It's giving your attention in a mindful, deliberate, conscious way."

Power Up: Savoring is the process of noticing the good, then identifying and absorbing the good feelings that emerge out of that awareness.

If you intend awesome, savoring is a way to get there. Here's how to do it.

1. **Stop and enjoy.** Next time you take a sip of water, savor the experience of the liquid rolling down your throat. Become mindful when you unwrap a piece of chocolate or watch your child dance or give someone a hug. Neuropsychologist Rick Hanson suggests you take a good fifteen seconds to enjoy the moment. That way you absorb the positive energy and hang on to the good feelings a bit longer. Next time you experience a good feeling, stop and let it settle in.

2. **Use all your senses.** Live with everything you've got— your senses of sight, smell, touch, taste, hearing, and even your intuitive sense. Next time you eat a piece of chocolate, go slowly and process the experience viscerally and emotionally. When you head to the gym for a workout, experience it with your eyes, ears, nose, skin, and tongue (the taste of cool water, salty perspiration on your lips). When you tap into your senses, you find more moments to savor.

3. **Focus on specific things.** Seek out specific small details to savor and allow them to lead you to others like a chain reaction. You may savor the experience of driving a car, for example, and connect to the freedom you feel when you drive through the neighborhood, and then marvel at the engineering behind the vehicle or the feel of the wind in your hair when you drive with the window down.

4. **Savor often.** There are countless opportunities to savor the moments of your life—the first sip of coffee in the morning, the smell of a tomato plant, a hug from a child, the sound of quiet, a deep breath. Focusing on the little moments that make up our days is actually more powerful than attaching to one big thing. Prioritize the practice. Bryant says it's also more powerful to notice ten little things during the day than to notice one big thing. It's the frequency of the practice that fuels the good feeling, not the intensity.

The better we become at savoring, at immersing ourselves in the feelings that come from noticing the good things in life, the more adept we become at experiencing beauty and joy.

....

IN THE MOMENT PRACTICE: LISTING YOUR LIKES

Savoring requires us to notice and process the moments of our lives by connecting to the emotions that well up when we experience something awesome or amazing or beautiful or marvelous.

Start to develop an awareness of your inner experience by noticing what you like and how it makes you feel.

Then, make a list to express or explain those feelings. Challenge yourself to come up with descriptive words to identify the experience. Get specific and consider words you may not ordinarily use: childlike, awesome, curious, wonder, exhilarating, *and so on. Have fun with this process of noticing and identifying.*

....

CREATING RITUALS TO BREAK THE ROUTINE

Rituals are another way to amp up the awe in our lives. They provide a structure for us to consciously open up to experience and move through it. This promotes a sense of calm and security that helps us process our experience.

Researchers Michael Norton and Francesca Gino found that any short ritual can defuse our feelings of upset, anger, and grief by providing a greater sense of control in that moment.

Funerals, for example, usually include some solemn and formal rituals that help us edge into our feelings of loss and gain support from others.

Same with singing "Happy Birthday" at a birthday party or "The Star-Spangled Banner" before a game—these rituals connect us, provide a sense that we are a part of something meaningful, rather than victims of random circumstance. They root us in the moment and enhance the experience.

Any set of repeated actions and procedures (usually more than one) that are performed in a meaningful or ceremonial way can be a ritual. I have a morning ritual. I start the day the same quiet way every morning. I sit on the edge of my bed, say a short prayer, give thanks, set an intention, and do some stretches before getting dressed.

Families also have their own rituals, particular ways of sitting down together for a meal or getting ready for bed or celebrating birthdays and other occasions.

Deliberate action through ritual can also be a powerful way to acknowledge and release the negative feelings around a personal setback, a failure or disappointment or loss. Struggling to let go? Create a ritual.

Write down your worries, then crumple up the paper and burn it or throw it away while saying, "I'm giving it up now."

You could also wash your hands, mindfully, or write out the bad feelings and bury them. Then plant new growth, a flower or seedling, in that spot.

A former teacher of mine smudges her workspace with sage and says a short blessing before starting work each day.

Whatever rituals you decide to create, just remember to include a few unique, significant, and repeatable steps. A couple of my favorites? Gratitude and a ritual of silence.

....

PERENNIAL PRACTICE: CREATE YOUR OWN RITUAL

Rituals enhance our lives by prompting us to become aware and connected to the present moment. Today, create your own ritual.

Identify a time of day when you become most stressed or feel disconnected, as though you are operating on autopilot. Then, design a three-step ritual around that time of day.

Consider when and where you will perform this ritual. It's best if it's performed in the same place each day.

Determine which actions you will take. Perhaps you'll mindfully make a cup of tea, or meditate, or stroll through the neighborhood. Decide how this ritual will begin and end.

Then, perform the ritual with focused attention and slow deliberate action. Do it every day for at least a week.

Journal about the experience. Does this ritual induce calm? Is it helping you to savor the little things in life? Is it enhancing your experience? If not, create another one that does.

....

GIVING THANKS

One of the most powerful rituals you can create is around gratitude. A regular gratitude practice helps us manage stress, make good on our goals, and feel better.

When I'm veering off course and getting caught up in the annoyances of modern-day life, like, say, the cable goes out or my computer is wonky, I stop myself and take part in a gratitude ritual. I stop what I'm doing, right then, and make a list of five or more things that I'm grateful for. After my list is complete, I reread each item on the list, take a deep breath, and allow feelings of gratitude to flow in. Then, aloud, I say "Thank you."

Another way to get your gratitude on is to stop and notice all those people who are helping to make your life easier. Right? We certainly notice those who cut in line, or are rude to us on the phone. But shift your focus to those who are adding to your life simply because they are doing what they do as well as they can do it—the teller at the bank, the bus driver, the school secretary, hairstylist, kids, partner, vet, bagger at the store, whoever. Pause, look into their eyes, and offer a sincere "Thank you." Not only will you feel better and grateful and good, but you will change their day too.

GET QUIET

Like gratitude, silence is sanity-producing. It gives me a sense of myself. Takes me out of rumination and ego and reminds me who I am—who we all are—beings of light and energy and love and awesome. Sometimes we've got to get out of the routine of doing and move into the place of being. Silence is the way.

Whether it's one minute each hour, an hour each day, or twenty minutes on the drive home from work, silence is a key component of recognizing the awesome within. Quiet time will help you bring all the frayed ends of your life back together.

When I settle into a quiet space, not only do I stop being so reactive, but often some thought, feeling, or insight emerges that changes the way I see myself and the world. It's as though all that stuff, the answers to life's big questions, is just sitting there waiting for us to quiet the background noise so it can be heard.

This is where magic emerges. Where love expands. Where peace wraps around you, warming you like an old cardigan. This is spiritual. And it is crazy reassuring and a fascinating act of self-discovery. If you are wigging out; feeling stressed; finding it hard to tune in, be aware, or believe that even an ounce of awesome exists in your life right now; get quiet and simply see what comes.

No matter how upsetting our situation, silence leads to insight and clarity and peace.

....

Live Well: *Take ten minutes for silence today. Sit in a quiet, nurturing spot. You can even relate to others through your silence. But do not speak or allow yourself to be distracted by computers or text messages or televisions or other external forces. Silence, too, the critical inner voices. Breathe the silence in, ground yourself in it. At the end of ten minutes, you'll feel calmer, more peaceful and more present.*

....

What? What's that? No time for quiet in your day? Here are some tips to silence the noise of life, at least for a minute.

1. **Put it on the calendar.** Schedule a period of silence. Pencil it in like a doctor's appointment. Make it a priority. Or build it in during the transitions of the day, after kitchen cleanup or during a lunch break.

2. **Create a ritual for quiet.** Go to the same place, at the same time, and start it the same way each time. I begin

with gratitude, then I grow silent. I do this for a few minutes at a time throughout my day. Prime yourself for silence by developing a ritual or habit that inspires peace and awareness.

3. **Be gentle.** Sometimes you'll hear nothing but your mind whining. Sometimes you'll be begging for insight on the meaning of life and get a dinner recipe. Cut yourself some slack. Don't judge. Be curious and relax. It might be the only break you take all day.

WATCH THE INNER CHIT-CHAT

When we settle down a bit and get quiet enough to hear ourselves think, we will also hear those inner voices gossiping about us. You know, the inner dialogue that says things like "Can you believe what she's wearing?" or "I've got to get the clothes in the dryer and remember to pick up the dry cleaning."

You will also hear a whole bunch of baloney like "You can't do that," "That's never going to work," and "Who do you think you are?"

Studies show that positive self-talk—encouraging phrases like "I think I can," "You can do it," and "You go, girl"—and those inner organizational reminders like "Pick up the milk" or "Take the fish out of the freezer" are a helpful and healthy way to support our experience.

Positive self-talk helps improve performance even more than visualization and other success-building strategies do, says researcher Randall Masciana. But those negative, critical, demeaning voices? Well, that stuff is just downright defeating.

So next time you hear that inner chatter—and you know you will—listen up. Then revise, rework, or delete anything that keeps you from attracting awesomeness into your life.

....

Be Awesome: *We can experience awe right now and create it in our lives and the lives of others by keeping our focus on the qualities we want to have in our lives. A mantra can help. Today, pick a power word ("Yes!") or phrase ("I am love," "I've got this," "I am joy," "This is awesome," or "Om," which, when said aloud, some say is the frequency of God). Repeat your mantra during a quiet two minutes, keeping your focus on that word or phrase. Then repeat it throughout your day during the challenging times and during those moments where you feel in flow. Use it to ground you, to remind you who you are, to attract the higher energy of awesome into your experience.*

....

GETTING LUCKY

When you put your intention out to the Universe and become deeply aware of your experience through silence and appreciation and other practices, good stuff is going to happen. Fun stuff. Great stuff. Amazing, awesome stuff. And you are going to feel lucky and fortunate and amazed.

Consistently lucky people are those who actually take on behaviors and habits that draw good things into their lives in the first place, says psychologist and author Richard Wiseman. They take on challenge with more of an optimistic, growth-oriented mindset; they see themselves as resilient and also believe themselves to be lucky. All of that leads to some super-cool mojo and "luckier" outcomes.

Power Up: Lucky people, those who seem to have fortunate things routinely happen to them, are usually those who engage in life in a big way. They are optimistic, curious, and grateful. Good things happen to those who believe good things are possible.

REPAIRING AND RESTORING

Until it doesn't. Until life smashes through the door, eats all your food, messes with your remote, and smacks you around before leaving you alone to cry in the corner. Despite our vast reserves of resilience and grit, despite our intellectual prowess and growth mindset, there will be moments, minutes, days when it all just falls apart. When you feel fully flawed and human and anything but awesome.

I hear you. Truly. Been there. Will be there again. So I say this from a place of love—get over it. We all have moments like this when the so-called little stuff causes us to crumble. You will survive it, but there are a couple of things you can do to help—and I mean a couple of things *other* than hitting every happy hour in the city.

One, this is a time to treat yourself, and others, gently. Put in for a little self-compassion. Be patient and kind to yourself. Laugh at the absurdity. And two, ground yourself again in who you know yourself to be: a creative higher energy. Light.

WORKING TOWARD AWESOME

Some days, it may take a little effort to remember your awesome. Some days when my kid is fighting me for the computer and the cat is throwing up and the bills are due and I still haven't finished the article and I'm feeling a little bit sick and sorry for myself, I need to take big, conscious, deliberate action to take me out of the awful and put me back in my awesome.

So I do that. Right? And you can too. Shoot, if I can do this stuff, people, anyone can. On the days when I'm feeling more dark than light, I go looking for the light. I seek out the goodness. It can be so subtle, so easy to overlook, but it's life-changing when we see it, when we realize the awe has been in there all the time.

Awesome exists in every moment. Whether you access it or not depends on what you notice. Just because people used to watch black and white televisions doesn't mean that color didn't exist in the world; we simply needed the technology to see it.

Accessing awesome is like that. It's all around you. It's within you. Living an awesome life, then, is about developing the personal mindsets, practices, rituals, and beliefs to help you see it.

You don't have to go away to do this. You don't need to spend any more time or money. You don't need a better education, house, or car. You simply need to develop habits that will give you an edge. Habits that will make it easier to see what is already before you and who you already are. Habits that create happiness and abundance and peace.

Be deliberate in your search for the good stuff, and when you catch it, when you feel it and notice it, let it in. Let it touch you and fill you up. Let it merge with your essence. No matter what is going on out there, out in that external realm of loss and traffic jams and bad sales calls and fattening foods, you can always choose to find the goodness. And there is no reason not to.

This is how to live an awesome life. And most days—even through the cancer and twelve-hundred-dollar car repairs and chronic illness and sassy kid and nights when I don't know what I'm going to cook and days when my husband forgets to run the dishwasher—I can still see awesome. Everywhere. My hope now is that perhaps you can see it too.

....

Night Cap: *As you settle into the evening, make a list of all the things you think are awesome, the things that move you or inspire you or make you well up with joy and gratitude. Just let them stream into your awareness. When we learn what awesome looks like, it shows up everywhere.*

....

ABOUT THE AUTHOR

POLLY CAMPBELL is a sought-after motivational speaker; the author of three books, *Imperfect Spirituality: Extraordinary Enlightenment for Ordinary People, How to Reach Enlightenment,* and *How to Live an Awesome Life.*

She is also a magazine writer and blogger and her work appears regularly in national publications such as *Spirituality & Health* and *Energy Times* magazines and on Web sites including Psychology Today, Psych Central, the Huffington Post, and others.

Campbell is a multitasking wife and mother who integrates the practices and strategies she writes and speaks about into her everyday life. She lives with her family in Oregon and seeks the awe in every moment.